BATTLE ZONE NORMANDY

JUNO
BEACH

The 'Battle Zone Normandy' Series

All of these titles can be ordered via the
Sutton Publishing website
www.suttonpublishing.co.uk

The 'Battle Zone Normandy'
Editorial and Design Team

Series Editor Simon Trew

Senior Commissioning Editor Jonathan Falconer

Assistant Editor Nick Reynolds

Cover and Page Design Martin Latham

Editing and Layout Donald Sommerville

Mapping Map Creation Ltd

Photograph Scanning and Mapping Bow Watkinson

Index Michael Forder

Battle Zone NORMANDY

JUNO BEACH

KEN FORD

Series Editor: Simon Trew

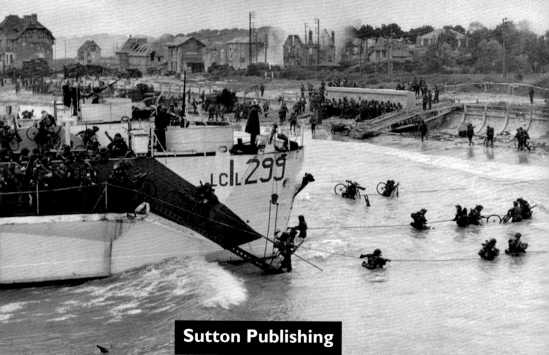

Sutton Publishing

First Published in 2004 by
Sutton Publishing Limited · Phoenix Mill
Thrupp · Stroud · Gloucestershire · GL5 2BU

British Library Cataloguing in Publication Data
A catalogue record for this book is available
from The British Library.

ISBN 0-7509-3007-1

Typeset in 10.5/14 pt Sabon

Printed and bound in England by
J.H. Haynes & Co. Ltd, Sparkford

Front cover: Commandos landing on Nan Red Beach. (*Imperial War Museum [IWM] B5218*)

Page 1: Restored Churchill AVRE on display near the spot where it met its demise just inland from Mike Red Beach. (*Author*)

Page 3: Nan White Beach at Bernières in the late morning of D-Day. In the centre, a bridge has been laid over the curved sea wall, opening an exit for wheeled traffic. (*National Archives of Canada [NAC] PA-131506*)

Page 7: Tanks moving forward past infantry of 8th Canadian Infantry Brigade. (*Lt H.G. Aikman, NAC PA-129128*)

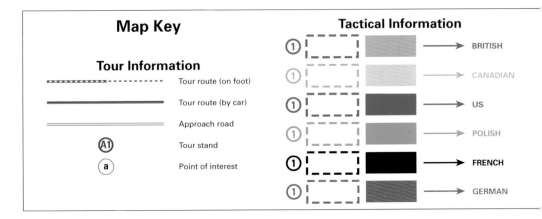

Map Key	Tactical Information
Tour Information	① ⬜ ▨ → BRITISH
▪▪▪▪▪▪▪▪▪▪▪▪▪▪▪ Tour route (on foot)	① ⬜ ▨ → CANADIAN
——————— Tour route (by car)	① ⬜ ▨ → US
═══════════ Approach road	① ⬜ ▨ → POLISH
(A1) Tour stand	① ⬜ ▨ → FRENCH
(a) Point of interest	① ⬜ ▨ → GERMAN

CONTENTS

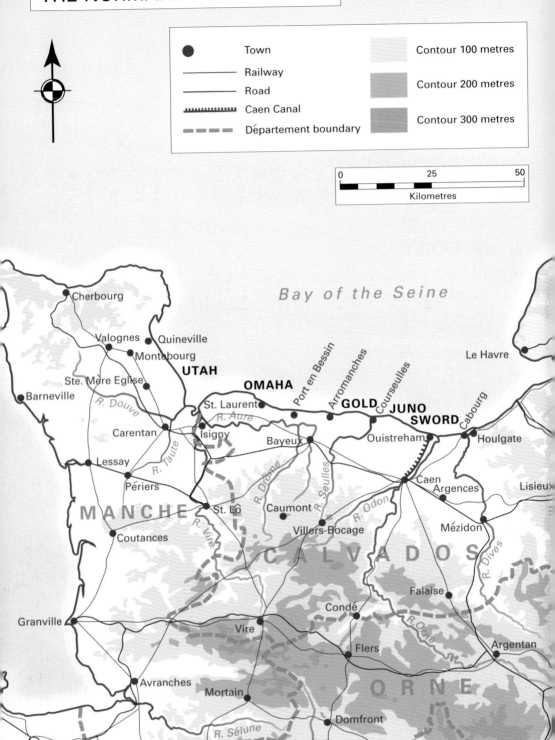

THE NORMANDY BATTLEFIELD

●	Town	Contour 100 metres
—	Railway	Contour 200 metres
—	Road	Contour 300 metres
⬤⬤⬤	Caen Canal	
– – –	Département boundary	

0   25   50

Kilometres

Bay of the Seine

Cherbourg

Valognes   Quineville

Montebourg

Ste. Mère Eglise   **UTAH**

Barneville

R. Douve   St. Laurent   **OMAHA**   Port en Bessin   Arromanches   Courseulles   Le Havre

GOLD   **JUNO**

SWORD

Carentan   Isigny   Bayeux   Ouistreham   Cabourg

R. Taute   *R. Aure*   Houlgate

Lessay   *R. Drôme*   *R. Seulles*   Caen   Argences

Périers   St. Lô   Caumont   *R. Odon*   Lisieux

MANCHE   *R. Vire*   Villers-Bocage   Mézidon

Coutances   **CALVADOS**

R. Dives

Falaise

Condé

Granville   Vire   *R. Orne*

Flers   Argentan

Avranches   **ORNE**

Mortain   Domfront

R. Sélune

R. Mayenne   Alençon

Fougères

PART ONE

INTRODUCTION

BATTLE ZONE NORMANDY

The Battle of Normandy was one of the greatest military clashes of all time. From late 1943, when the Allies appointed their senior commanders and began the air operations that were such a vital preliminary to the invasion, until the end of August 1944, it pitted against one another several of the most powerful nations on earth, as well as some of their most brilliant minds. When it was won, it changed the world forever. The price was high, but for anybody who values the principles of freedom and democracy, it is difficult to conclude that it was one not worth paying.

I first visited Lower Normandy in 1994, a year after I joined the War Studies Department at the Royal Military Academy Sandhurst (RMAS). With the 50th anniversary of D-Day

Royal Marines from 48 RM Commando talk to French civilians in St-Aubin on 7 June with a Centaur tank from 2nd Royal Marine Armoured Support Regiment in the background. *(Author's collection)*

Rear view of the battle-scarred 50-mm gun casemate on the edge of Mike Red Beach, close by the western side of the harbour entrance at Courseulles. The prevailing winds and shifting sands are causing the concrete structure gradually to slip beneath the dunes. *(Author)*

looming, it was decided that the British Army would be represented at several major ceremonies by one of the RMAS's officer cadet companies. It was also suggested that the cadets should visit some of the battlefields, not least to bring home to them the significance of why they were there. Thus, at the start of June 1994, I found myself as one of a small team of military and civilian directing staff flying with the cadets in a draughty and noisy Hercules transport to visit the beaches and fields of Calvados, in my case for the first time.

I was hooked. Having met some of the veterans and seen the ground over which they fought – and where many of their friends died – I was determined to go back. Fortunately, the Army encourages battlefield touring as part of its soldiers' education, and on numerous occasions since 1994 I have been privileged to return to Normandy, often to visit new sites. In the process I have learned a vast amount, both from my colleagues (several of whom are contributors to this series) and from my enthusiastic and sometimes tri-service audiences, whose professional insights and penetrating questions have frequently made me re-examine my own assumptions and prejudices. Perhaps inevitably,

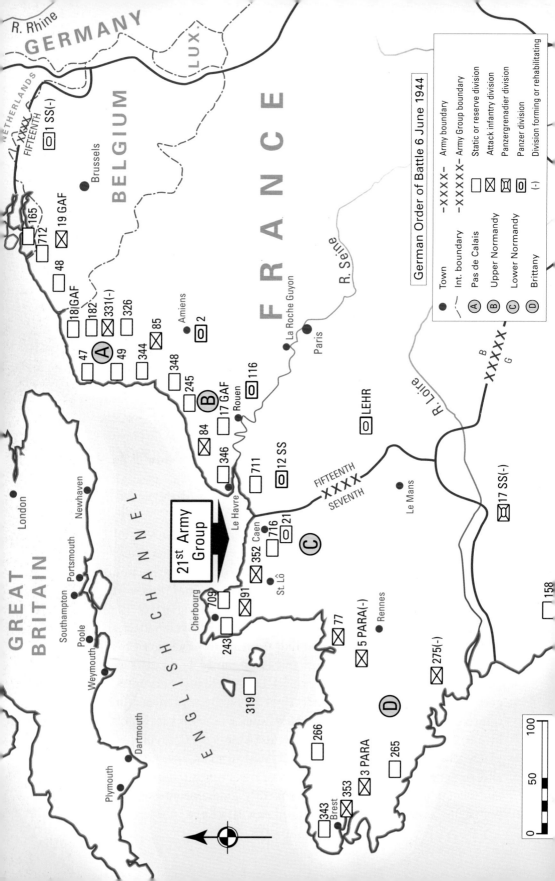

especially when standing in one of Normandy's beautifully-maintained Commonwealth War Graves Commission cemeteries, I have also found myself deeply moved by the critical events that took place there in the summer of 1944.

Panther tank from 1st Company, 12th SS Panzer Regiment, destroyed in the German attack on Bretteville-l'Orgueilleuse on 8–9 June. This tank was knocked out on the road to the south of the town by anti-tank fire and has been rolled over off the road by engineers to clear the way. *(IWM B6053)*

'Battle Zone Normandy' was conceived by Jonathan Falconer, Commissioning Editor at Sutton Publishing, in 2001. Why not, he suggested, bring together recent academic research – some of which challenges the general perception of what happened on and after 6 June 1944 – with a perspective based on familiarity with the ground itself? We agreed that the opportunity existed for a series that would set out to combine detailed and accurate narratives, based mostly on primary sources, with illustrated guides to the ground itself, which could be used either in the field (sometimes quite literally), or by the armchair explorer. The book in your hands is the product of that agreement.

The 'Battle Zone Normandy' series consists of 14 volumes, covering most of the major and many of the minor engagements that went together to create the Battle of Normandy. The first six books deal with the airborne and amphibious landings on 6 June

The main entrance to Ardennes abbey. The Regina Rifles finally captured the buildings in the early hours of 9 July. *(Author)*

1944, and with the struggle to create the firm lodgement that was the prerequisite for eventual Allied victory. Five further volumes cover some of the critical battles that followed, as the Allies' plans unravelled and they were forced to improvise a battle very different from that originally intended. Finally, the last three titles in the series examine the fruits of the bitter attritional struggle of June and July 1944, as the Allies irrupted through the German lines or drove them back in fierce fighting. The series ends, logically enough, with the devastation of the German armed forces in the 'Falaise Pocket' in late August.

Whether you use these books while visiting Normandy, or to experience the battlefields vicariously, we hope you will find them as interesting to read as we did to research and write. Far from the inevitable victory that is sometimes represented, D-Day and the ensuing battles were full of hazards and unpredictability. Contrary to the view often expressed, had the invasion failed, it is far from certain that a second attempt could have been mounted. Remember this, and the significance of the contents of this book, not least for your life today, will be the more obvious.

Dr Simon Trew
Royal Military Academy Sandhurst
December 2003

PART TWO

HISTORY

CHAPTER I

OPERATION OVERLORD AND JUNO BEACH

The assault landings made by 3rd Canadian Infantry Division over Juno Beach in the early morning of 6 June 1944 were the culmination of four long years of training, exercising and waiting for the moment when it would be called forward to play its part in the liberation of the Nazi-occupied territories. The return of Allied forces to the mainland of Europe had been a long time in coming and the Canadian troops who had been garrisoning the British Isles for almost four years were straining for a chance to engage the enemy in battle.

Above: General Sir Bernard Montgomery arrives in France on 8 June. His landing took place on Mike Red Beach (part of the Juno area), close by the exit that led inland to Graye-sur-Mer. *(IWM B5174)*

Page 13: Royal Marines from 4th Special Service Brigade HQ arrive on Nan Red Beach in the small Landing Craft Infantry – LCI(S) – that has carried them over the Channel. The steep ramps leading down from the light wooden craft made disembarkation very difficult. Many men were tipped into the sea as the ends of the walkways bucked violently on the incoming waves. *(IWM B5219)*

Above: Commandos receive last minute orders in their transit camp on Southampton Common prior to embarkation for France. *(IWM H38948)*

After long deliberation, the Allied planners chose Lower Normandy as the site of the landings. The area was something of a compromise solution, and was selected for a number of reasons. The shortest route over the Channel from England to France and then into Germany was across the Straits of Dover, with a landing in the Pas de Calais. The close proximity of the area to Britain would allow fighter aircraft based near the English coast to provide continuous air cover to the assault. But this route was also an obvious one to the Germans, who took the precaution of fortifying the coastline along this part of northern France with massive defensive works and coastal gun batteries.

Ultimately, Lower Normandy was chosen as offering the best prospects of success. It was close enough to allow air cover for the assault, albeit of reduced duration as the fighters would have to make a 500-kilometre (km) round trip from their bases in England. The coastal defences, although impressive, were believed to be not as deep and well completed as those around Calais. The proposed landing beaches were also reasonably close to the ports of Cherbourg and Le Havre, although the Allies intended to transport their own ports with them in the shape of prefabricated 'Mulberry' harbours. There was also an extensive road network radiating from Caen in the eastern sector of the landings with good routes to the south over flat countryside, which would be excellent for the deployment of armoured forces.

Once the choice of landing area had been made, the overall plan could be developed. In the west, US 4th Infantry Division would land on Utah Beach at the south-eastern end of the Cotentin Peninsula. US 82nd and 101st Airborne Divisions, which were to drop in the early hours before the amphibious landings, would secure the inland exits off the beach and key strategic road junctions and bridges. On 4th Infantry Division's left flank, regimental combat teams from US 1st and 29th Infantry Divisions would assault Omaha Beach, to the east of the estuary of the River Vire. Their task was to join up with the landings on either side to form a continuous beachhead, then to push to the south. In the extreme east of the landings, 3rd British Infantry Division would land close by the River Orne over Sword Beach, with its left flank protected by 6th British Airborne Division which would have arrived by parachute and glider during the night. The task of 3rd British Infantry Division, one of the most important of the whole Allied plan, was to advance inland with all speed and capture Caen.

In the centre of these three landings two further divisions would attack, 50th (Northumbrian) Division on Gold Beach and 3rd Canadian Infantry Division on Juno. These two divisions would form a solid centre to the landings, linking up with the flanking divisions to form a lodgement through which follow-up forces would deploy. In the centre of all this, the Canadians landing over Juno Beach would stake out their own bridgehead and then attack southwards to take the high ground west of Caen and the airfield at Carpiquet, keeping abreast of 3rd British Infantry Division during its advance to capture Caen itself.

Juno Beach, 3rd Canadian Infantry Division's landing point, was composed of a number of wide sandy beaches centred on the small fishing port of Courseulles-sur-Mer. They stretched from a point just to the east of la Rivière across to Luc-sur-Mer and were designated, from west to east, Love, Mike and Nan. In turn, each of these was subdivided into sectors labelled Green, White and Red. The assault landings were set to take place on just a small part of the whole Juno Beach. 7th Canadian Infantry Brigade was

Canadian soldiers at a captured German HQ study a model of the Nan Green and Mike Red beach defences on either side of Courseulles. *(Ken Bell, NAC PA-131438)*

to land astride the estuary of the River Seulles at Courseulles over Mike Green and Red Beaches and Nan Green, while 8th Canadian Infantry Brigade planned to assault at Bernières-sur-Mer across Nan White and Nan Red. There were to be no landings on Love Beach.

The seaward approach to these beaches was over a complicated series of rocky ledges stretching for some 2 km parallel to the shore. These shallows would be covered at high tide but posed a considerable threat to incoming craft at H-Hour, the time that the assault troops would hit the beach. This was because this time was set to be when the tide reached its midway point. To guard against the landing craft striking these natural

The monument and Norman house by the main exit in the middle of Nan White Beach. The house was the first to be liberated in Normandy by the Canadians and has a plaque to this effect outside on the promenade. It appears in many of the contemporary pictures of the landings. Maj-Gen Keller arrived here with his advance HQ and exited the beach at this point. *(Author)*

obstacles, the landings on Juno were delayed by 15 minutes, allowing for a greater depth of water to be provided by the incoming tide. This meant that the Canadians would be arriving after the assaults had gone in over Gold and Sword Beaches. By then the Germans would be alerted to the arrival of the invasion.

3rd Canadian Infantry Division's objectives were divided into four phases. Initially, the division was to break through the coastal defences to establish itself in the three seaside villages of Courseulles, Bernières and St-Aubin-sur-Mer along a phase line code-named 'Yew' some 2 km inland. The next phase line was called 'Elm', 9 km from the beaches. This was the intermediate objective for the follow-up battalions. They would have to seize crossings over the Rivers Seulles and Mue and take various villages including Pierrepont, Colomby-sur-Thaon and Anguerny. The reserve formation, 9th Canadian Infantry Brigade, was to land on Nan Beach and then move on to phase line 'Oak', to the west of Caen 16 km from the landings. This line ran along the route of the Caen–Bayeux highway and overlooked Carpiquet airfield. The final phase then envisaged a reorganisation along the Oak line to meet the anticipated German counter-attack.

The right flank of the Canadian attack would be just 1 km to the east of the landings to be made by 50th (Northumbrian) Division over Gold Beach. Contact between the two divisions would be established immediately after the landings. On the left of the Canadians, 3rd British Infantry Division would be landing more than 7 km to the east over Sword Beach. No landings could be made within this wide gap because of the offshore shoals. Two British commandos would therefore be landed to link together Sword and Juno Beaches. No. 48 Royal Marine (RM) Commando would land with the Canadians and move east; No. 41 RM Commando would land on Sword and move west. They aimed to meet up in the hamlet of Petit Enfer.

The Canadian advance inland to phase line Oak was planned to be in line with 3rd British Infantry Division's drive for Caen. It was important that the two divisions keep abreast of each other to provide mutual support. Once the Canadians were established around the area of Carpiquet airfield to the west of Caen, they could then strike eastwards to help capture the city or south-eastwards to cut off the rear of Caen and to establish a bridgehead over the River Orne to the south of the city. Caen's early capture was vital to future Allied strategy in Normandy.

CHAPTER 2

OPPOSING COMMANDERS AND THEIR FORCES

The great crusade to free Europe from the Nazis was led by an American, General Dwight D. Eisenhower, Supreme Commander Allied Expeditionary Force, although the bulk of the forces taking part in the initial attack were from Britain and the Commonwealth. Eisenhower was probably the best suited for this post of all the Allied commanders. He embodied the very spirit of Allied co-operation and also had considerable experience in amphibious warfare, having been overall commander for the landings in North Africa, Sicily and Italy. Air Chief Marshal (ACM) Sir Arthur Tedder was designated as Eisenhower's deputy, with General Sir Bernard Montgomery, commander of 21st Army

Group, heading all land forces – British, Canadian and American – which were to be used in the invasion. Montgomery was the most experienced and successful of all the British land commanders available. He did, however, have his critics and was often seen as a very difficult and outspoken individual to deal with. Many American and some British commanders openly detested him. The air component of the invasion, the Allied Expeditionary Air Force, was under the command of ACM Sir Trafford Leigh-Mallory. Leading the naval part of the operation (Operation 'Neptune') was Admiral Sir Bertram Ramsay.

Two armies were to land over Utah, Omaha, Gold, Juno and Sword Beaches on 6 June: British Second Army, commanded by Lieutenant-General (Lt-Gen) Miles Dempsey; and First US Army, under the command of Lieutenant General Omar Bradley. The overall objective during the first 24 hours after the landings was to carve out a beachhead 80 km long and 16 km deep from east of the River Orne to Pont l'Abbé on the Cotentin Peninsula, to include the major towns of Caen and Bayeux. In the centre of this lodgement was Juno Beach.

Juno and Sword Beaches were allocated to I British Corps for its landings. Commanding I British Corps was Lt-Gen John Crocker, a veteran of the First World War and a long serving

Lt-Gen Miles Dempsey (*left*), commander of British Second Army, talking with Maj-Gen Percy Hobart, commander of 79th Armoured Division. 79th Armoured Division never fought as a unit, but provided specialised armoured vehicles to tackle fortifications and obstacles wherever they were needed. (*IWM H38215*)

HISTORY

member of the Royal Tank Regiment. Commander of a brigade in France in 1940 and then a corps in Tunisia in 1943, he then returned to Britain to train I British Corps for the invasion.

In July 1943, 3rd Canadian Infantry Division was selected for the invasion under the command of Major-General (Maj-Gen) Rod Keller. For the next year Keller trained his division specifically for this one event, undertaking a series of exercises with the naval forces that would carry his unit ashore. Keller had gained rapid promotion after arriving in Britain with the Canadian forces in December 1940, rising from major to major-general in just two years, mainly due to the confidence shown in him by I Canadian Corps' commander, Lt-Gen Henry Crerar. Keller was 44 years of age when he led his division into action on D-Day. He was too young to have seen service in the First World War and was yet to see action in the current conflict.

In June 1944, 3rd Canadian Infantry Division was an all-volunteer force. None of the men who landed in the Canadian assault waves on D-Day had been conscripted to serve overseas. When war began Canada had just a small regular army of only 4,500 professional soldiers. The mobilisation of the militia regiments, however, soon allowed the forming of several divisions for overseas service. 3rd Canadian Infantry Division was sent to

Maj-Gen Keller (*left*) in discussion with Lt-Gen Crocker, commander of I British Corps, in the days following the landings. (*Frank L. Dubervill, NAC PA-190502*)

the UK in the spring of 1941 and remained there in training until it left for Normandy three years later.

Nine battalions of infantry made up 3rd Canadian Infantry Division; all of them were militia regiments and each had its own history and traditions. They were formed into three brigades, as detailed in the accompanying order of battle (*see pages 26–27*).

For the D-Day invasion, the firepower of the division's three field regiments of the Royal Canadian Artillery (RCA) was augmented by the 19th Field Regiment, RCA. All of these units were equipped with Priest

105-mm self-propelled guns. The manoeuvrability of these weapons allowed them to move into position quickly once ashore, and they could also fire in support of the landings while still aboard the tank landing craft bringing them to the beaches.

Canadian troops training in the art of street fighting amongst the bombed-out buildings of Southampton. The Regina Rifles were confronted with this type of fighting immediately on arrival in Normandy, when the leading companies had to clear houses in Courseulles before they could advance inland. (NAC PA-162247)

The Allies knew that the Germans had fortified all of the beaches of Lower Normandy. The beaches were covered with obstacles and explosives between the high and low water marks, all sited so as to sink or damage approaching landing craft. Welded sections of railway lines, steel and concrete tetrahedrons, stakes topped with mines, and complicated steel traps littered the sands. All of these would have to be neutralised or avoided. Parties of British and Canadian Royal Engineers would land with the main assault to try to blast paths through the obstacles ahead of other incoming landing craft. The timing of the assault would be midway between low and high tides. This would leave many of the defences exposed and avoidable. It would also mean a relatively narrow width of open beach for the infantry to cross before they got to the German defences. At the top of the beaches a triple belt of barbed wire had been laid to tie together the fortifications, with minefields laid out behind. Machine-gun and mortar posts, housed in small concrete 'Tobruk' emplacements and open nests, were sited to fire along the length of the beaches. Anchoring these lines of field defences were larger strongpoints with heavier weapons. These usually had 6–10 machine guns, several 81-mm mortars, and one or two 50-mm anti-tank guns. Some had larger weapons, often 75-mm and 88-mm guns. All were housed in concrete bunkers or casemates. These strongpoints were called *Wiederstandnester* (WN) or 'resistance nests' and were placed about 2,000 metres apart, sited to provide mutual support and to cover routes inland from the beach.

At the crucial moment when the Canadian infantry actually touched down on Juno Beach, they would not be facing these strong enemy defences alone. Landing just before them, already in action, would be the tanks of the supporting armoured brigade and the specialised equipment of 79th British Armoured Division. Great thought and ingenuity had been given to getting armoured vehicles up to the defences in front of the infantry, so that when the infantry arrived Allied armour would have already engaged the defenders at close quarters. It was hoped that this brief respite from aimed fire would allow the Canadians to get across the beach and into the fortifications that lined the top of the shore.

One solution used to get armour on the beach at the right moment was the deployment of Duplex Drive (DD) tanks. These tanks were made buoyant by means of a thick canvas screen and were pushed through the water by two propellers. Once afloat they had the advantage of a very low freeboard and were difficult for the enemy to see, but they could not fire their guns when they were swimming. It was planned to launch these amphibious tanks a few thousand metres out from the shore from where they would 'swim' unnoticed to the landing beach and then emerge from the surf just before the assault boats carrying the infantry touched down. On dry land the DD Shermans would drop their skirts, disengage their propeller drives and function as normal tanks, tackling the enemy as the infantry stormed ashore. On 7th Canadian Infantry Brigade's front, the DD tanks of 6th Canadian Armoured Regiment (1st Hussars) would lead the assault, while 10th Canadian Armoured Regiment (The Fort Garry Horse) would land on 8th Canadian Infantry Brigade's beaches.

The 79th Armoured Division was to provide other specialised armour for the landings on Juno Beach. Equipment especially designed for the assault had been under development in Britain for a long period. Tank experts had studied the problems

Order of Battle 3rd Canadian Infantry Division
6 June 1944

General Officer Commanding	**Maj-Gen R.F.L. Keller**

7th Canadian Infantry Brigade — *Brig H.W. Foster*
- The Royal Winnipeg Rifles — *Lt-Col J.M. Meldram*
- The Regina Rifles Regiment — *Lt-Col F.M. Matheson*
- 1st Battalion, The Canadian Scottish Regiment — *Lt-Col F.N. Cabeldu*

8th Canadian Infantry Brigade — *Brig K.G. Blackader*
- The Queen's Own Rifles of Canada — *Lt-Col J.G. Spragge*
- Le Régiment de la Chaudière — *Lt-Col J.E.G.P. Mathieu*
- The North Shore (New Brunswick) Regiment — *Lt-Col D.B. Buell*

9th Canadian Infantry Brigade — *Brig D.G. Cunningham*
- The Highland Light Infantry of Canada — *Lt-Col F.M. Griffiths*
- The Stormont, Dundas & Glengarry Highlanders — *Lt-Col G.H. Christiansen*
- The North Nova Scotia Highlanders — *Lt-Col C. Petch*

Divisional Troops

Reconnaissance
- 7th Reconnaissance Regt (17th Duke of York's Royal Canadian Hussars)

Machine Gun and Heavy Mortar Battalion
- The Cameron Highlanders of Ottawa

Royal Canadian Artillery — **Brig P.A.S. Todd**
- 12th Field Regt – 14th, 16th and 43rd Field Btys — *Lt-Col R.H. Webb*
- 13th Field Regt – 22nd, 44th and 78th Field Btys — *Lt-Col Clifford*
- 14th Field Regt – 34th, 66th and 81st Field Btys — *Lt-Col H.S. Griffin*
- 3rd Anti-Tank Regiment
- 4th Light Anti-Aircraft Regiment

Royal Canadian Engineers — *Lt-Col R.J. Cassidy*
- 6th Field Company
- 16th Field Company
- 18th Field Company

Royal Canadian Signals — *Lt-Col G.O. Gamble*
- 3rd Canadian Infantry Division Signals

Royal Canadian Army Medical Corps
- 14th Canadian Field Ambulance
- 22nd Canadian Field Ambulance
- 23rd Canadian Field Ambulance

Attached Armoured Support

2nd Canadian Armoured Brigade — *Brig R.A. Wyman*
- 6th Cdn Armoured Regt (1st Hussars) — *Lt-Col L.R.J. Colwell*
- 10th Cdn Armoured Regt (Fort Garry Horse) — *Lt-Col R.E. Morton*
- 27th Cdn Armoured Regt (Sherbrooke Fusiliers) — *Lt-Col M.B. Gordon*

Formations Attached for the Assault

4th Special Service Brigade
- No. 48 Royal Marine Commando — *Lt-Col J.L. Moulton*

Royal Marines
  3rd Armoured Support Battery
  4th Armoured Support Battery
Royal Armoured Corps
  C Squadron, The Inns of Court Regiment
Engineers (RE and RCE)
  26th and 80th Assault Squadrons, 5th Assault Regiment, RE
  71st and 262nd Field Companies, RE
  5th Field Company, RCE
Artillery (RCA and RA)
  19th Field Regiment, RCA – 55th, 63rd and 99th Field Batteries
  62nd Anti-Tank Regiment, RA – 245th and 248th Batteries
  73rd Light Anti-Aircraft Regiment, RA – 218th and 220th Batteries
  93rd Light Anti-Aircraft Regiment, RA – 321st Battery
  114th Light Anti-Aircraft Regiment, RA – 372nd and 375th Batteries
  474th Searchlight Battery, RA
  A Flight, 652nd Air Observation Point Squadron

102nd Beach Sub-Area, 7th and 8th Beach Groups
(under command for assault phase)
Beach Protection Infantry
  8th Battalion, The King's Regiment (Liverpool)
  5th Battalion, The Royal Berkshire Regt (Princess Charlotte of Wales')
Royal Engineers
  72nd, 85th, 184th and 240th Field Companies
  19th and 20th Stores Sections
  59th Mechanised Equipment Section
  11th and 1034th Port Operation Companies
  966th Inland Water Transport Operating Company
Royal Army Service Corps
  30th Transport Column
  199th and 282nd Transport Companies
  139th and 140th Detail Issue Depot
  240th and 242nd Petrol Depots
Medical
  32nd Casualty Clearing Station
  1st, 2nd, 32nd and 34th Field Dressing Stations
Ordnance
  15th Ordnance Beach Detachment
  45th Ordnance Ammunition Company
Royal Electrical and Mechanical Engineers
  22nd and 23rd Beach Recovery Sections
Provost
  242nd and 244th Provost Companies
Pioneer Corps
  58th, 115th, 144th, 170th, 190th, 225th, 243rd and 293rd Pioneer
  Companies

encountered by Canadian forces during the abortive raid on Dieppe in August 1942 and had proposed solutions to overcome them. A range of adaptations was applied to the Churchill tank to produce a vehicle capable of tackling highly specialised tasks.

Field Marshal von Rundstedt, OB West, visits 12th SS Panzer Division *Hitlerjugend* before the invasion. The picture shows, from left to right, von Rundstedt; *SS-Standartenführer* Kurt Meyer, commander of 25th SS Panzergrenadier Regiment; *SS-Brigadeführer* Fritz Witt, the divisional commander; and *SS-Gruppenführer* 'Sepp' Dietrich, commander of I SS Panzer Corps. *(Bundesarchiv 1011/297/1739/16A)*

Manned by Royal Engineers (RE), the resulting tank was called an Assault Vehicle Royal Engineers (AVRE). To attack casemates and pill-boxes, the petard tank was developed. It was armed with a short-barrelled spigot mortar capable of firing a heavy block-busting charge against reinforced concrete buildings, shattering the structures with a devastating blast. The AVRE was also capable of other support functions, such as laying box-girder bridges, dropping fascines into anti-tank ditches, and putting down rolls of matting to form roadways across soft ground.

Manning the AVREs in support of 3rd Canadian Infantry Division would be 26th and 80th Squadrons, 5th Assault Regiment, Royal Engineers. 79th Armoured Division gave more support in the shape of flail tanks, known as 'Crabs'. These were Sherman gun tanks with a revolving drum anchored to the front on which was attached a number of heavy chains. They were designed to clear minefields. As the tank went forwards with the drum turning, the chains beat the ground ahead of it, exploding any mines in its path. B Squadron, 22nd Dragoons, and A Squadron, 2nd County of London Yeomanry (The Westminster Dragoons), provided this mine-clearing support to 3rd Canadian Infantry Division.

Field Marshal Erwin Rommel, commander of Army Group B. (IWM HU17183)

The lessons learned from the Dieppe raid stressed that there was a need for overwhelming fire power during the initial stages of the assault, much heavier than anything tried previously. A programme of bombing by the Royal Air Force (RAF) and US Army Air Force (USAAF) would be implemented well before the date of the invasion to help isolate Normandy. Rail lines and marshalling yards were to be attacked and bridges over rivers and canals destroyed. This disturbance of the Germans' transport infrastructure would slow down the rate at which they could send reinforcements into the invasion area. More immediate assistance to the land forces was to be provided through the aircraft of the two tactical air forces – the RAF's 2nd TAF assisting British Second Army, and the USAAF's Ninth AF helping First US Army. Fortifications, anti-tank obstacles, troop concentrations and batteries were all targets for Allied fighter-bombers. Strategic bombers were also to play their part, with RAF Bomber Command and the US Eighth Air Force bombing whole areas adjacent to the landing beaches.

Naval support for the invasion was to be equally impressive. A total of over 7,000 vessels would be involved, made up of 1,206 naval units, 4,127 landing craft of all types, 423 ancillary craft and 1,260 merchant ships. The American beaches, Utah and Omaha, were to be supported by the Western Task Force (Rear-Admiral Alan G. Kirk, USN) and the British beaches, Gold, Juno and Sword, by the Eastern Task Force (Rear-Admiral Sir Philip Vian, RN). Naval Force J, commanded by Commodore G.N. Oliver, would bring the Canadians across the Channel and blast them ashore. The naval bombardment was to be provided by

HISTORY

Bombardment Force E, which consisted of the cruisers *Diadem* and *Belfast*, together with 11 destroyers. Nor was this all, for attached to the assault flotillas during the run-in to the beach would be six Landing Craft Gun (Large) [LCG(L)], four Landing Craft Flak (LCF) and eight Landing Craft Rocket [LCT(R)], all pounding the shore with their various weapons. In addition, Landing Craft Assault (Hedgerow) [LCA(HR)] would each fire 24 x 60-pound bombs to clear lanes through wire and anti-personnel minefields and the division's own self-propelled guns would be firing from the open decks of their landing craft.

Naval Bombardment Force, Juno Beach

Flag officer: Rear-Admiral R.A. Dalrymple-Hamilton

Ship	Main guns	Target
HMS *Belfast* (cruiser)	12 x 6-in	WN-32 (in Gold Beach area)
HMS *Diadem* (cruiser)	8 x 5.25-in	100-mm battery at Bény
HMS *Kempenfelt* (destroyer)	4 x 4.7-in	battery behind Bernières
HMS *Venus* (destroyer)	4 x 4.7-in	Mike Beach defences
HMS *Faulknor* (destroyer)	5 x 4.7-in	Mike Beach defences
HMS *Fury* (destroyer)	4 x 4.7-in	Mike and Nan Green defences
HMS *Stevenstone* (destroyer)	4 x 4-in	Mike and Nan Green defences
FF *la Combattante* (destroyer)	4 x 4-in	Mike and Nan defences
HMS *Vigilant* (destroyer)	4 x 4.7-in	Langrune defences
HMCS *Algonquin* (destroyer)	4 x 4.7-in	St-Aubin defences
HMCS *Sioux* (destroyer)	4 x 4.7-in	St-Aubin defences
HMS *Bleasdale* (destroyer)	4 x 4-in	Nan Red and White defences
HNorMS *Glaisdale* (destroyer)	4 x 4-in	Nan Red and White defences

In contrast to the Allies' great show of strength at sea and in the air, the German Navy (*Kriegsmarine*) and Air Force (*Luftwaffe*) could muster little in reply. The Channel had been swept of all *Kriegsmarine* vessels, especially U-boats, save for some small coastal ships, minesweepers and torpedo boats holed up in various ports. *Admiral* Theodore Krancke, C-in-C Naval Group Command West, could only muster 103 light craft between Cherbourg and Boulogne. In the air, *Generalfeldmarschall* (Field Marshal) Hugo Sperrle, commander of 3rd Air Fleet, had only 115 serviceable single-engined fighters with which to protect the whole of France, Belgium and Holland.

The German command structure in France was convoluted. North-west France, including Normandy, was defended by Seventh Army, commanded by *Generaloberst* (Colonel-General) Friedrich Dollmann. Together with Fifteenth Army, Seventh Army formed part of Field Marshal Erwin Rommel's Army Group B, which in turn came under the command of Field Marshal Gerd von Rundstedt, Commander-in-Chief West (OB West). Rundstedt reported directly to the German Armed Forces High Command (OKW), which in reality meant Hitler himself. The sector in which the landings were to be carried out was held by LXXXIV Corps under *General der Artillerie* (General of Artillery) Erich Marcks. None of these officers was in a position to exercise complete command; most decisions had to be referred upwards, even minor ones sometimes going all the way to Hitler.

Opposing the Canadians along Juno Beach was part of 716th Infantry Division, commanded by *Generalleutnant* (GenLt) Wilhelm Richter. Richter's division was one of a number of static divisions raised in 1941 to perform coastal defence duties. It contained just two regiments, 726th and 736th Grenadier Regiments, each originally composed of three battalions. In early 1944 these two regiments were each supplemented by the addition of a further battalion. 439th *Ost* Battalion joined 726th Grenadier Regiment and 642nd *Ost* Battalion was added to 736th Grenadier Regiment. The *Ost* battalions were made up of captured troops from the Soviet Union, pressed into fighting for Germany in preference to risking their lives in the harsh prisoner of war camps. The Allies considered these extra troops to be of a poor calibre and likely to be of low morale.

German strategy to counter an invasion relied heavily on the strength of the coastal defences of Hitler's vaunted 'Atlantic Wall'. The success gained in pinning down Canadian troops and tanks on the beach at Dieppe led some Germans to believe that a strongly fortified shoreline could again stall an invasion from the sea. Rommel believed that the best place to defeat an invasion was on the beach. He advocated that a strong counter-attack be made by armoured forces as soon as the Allies came ashore, catching them exposed as they struggled to form a beachhead. To do this, he wanted the reserve panzer divisions located within striking distance of the coast. Other commanders felt that the armoured divisions should be held back to strike an annihilating blow at a time and place of their choosing when the Allies moved inland. In the event, Hitler tried to agree with both strategies and fudged the matter by leaving three panzer divisions close to the coast of northern France under Rommel's command and locating the others further inland with orders that they were not to be

HISTORY

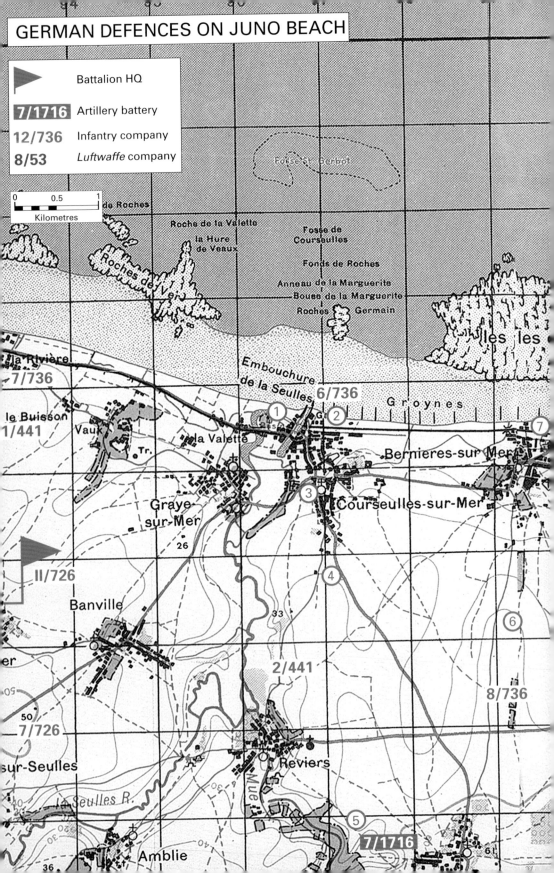

GERMAN DEFENCES ON JUNO BEACH

Battalion HQ

7/1716   Artillery battery

12/736   Infantry company

8/53   *Luftwaffe* company

0   0.5   1
Kilometres

Fosse St. Serbot

de Roches
Roche de la Valette
la Hure
de Veaux

Fosse de
Courseulles

Roches de Ver

Fonds de Roches

Anneau de la Marguerite

Bouse de la Marguerite

Roches   Germain

les   les

la Rivière
7/736

Embouchure
de la Seulles   **6/736**

G r o y n e s

le Buisson
1/441

Vaux

Tr.

la Valette

①   ②

⑦

Bernieres-sur-Mer

Graye-
sur-Mer

26

③

Courseulles-sur-Mer

II/726

Banville

④

33

⑥

2/441

8/736

7/726

sur-Seulles

la Seulles R.

Reviers

la Mue R.

⑤

7/1716

Amblie

36

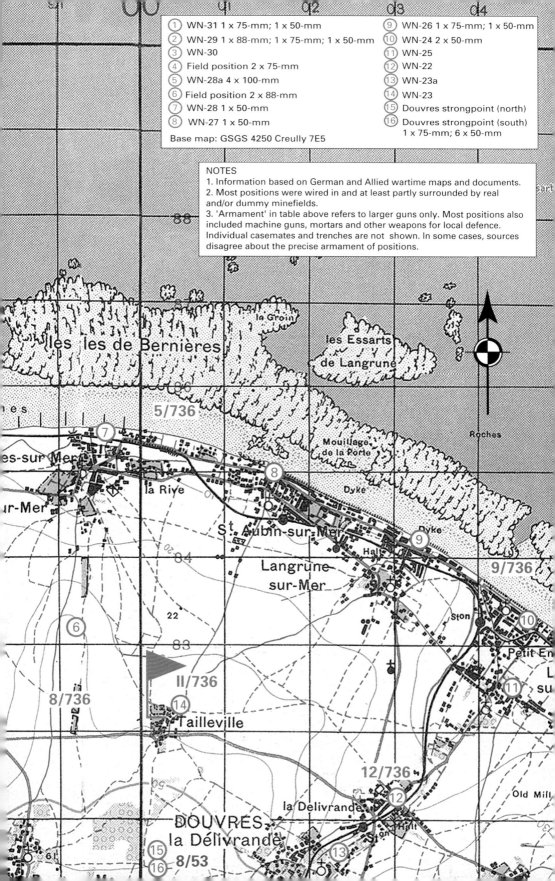

① WN-31 1 x 75-mm; 1 x 50-mm
② WN-29 1 x 88-mm; 1 x 75-mm; 1 x 50-mm
③ WN-30
④ Field position 2 x 75-mm
⑤ WN-28a 4 x 100-mm
⑥ Field position 2 x 88-mm
⑦ WN-28 1 x 50-mm
⑧ WN-27 1 x 50-mm
⑨ WN-26 1 x 75-mm; 1 x 50-mm
⑩ WN-24 2 x 50-mm
⑪ WN-25
⑫ WN-22
⑬ WN-23a
⑭ WN-23
⑮ Douvres strongpoint (north)
⑯ Douvres strongpoint (south)
  1 x 75-mm; 6 x 50-mm

Base map: GSGS 4250 Creully 7E5

NOTES
1. Information based on German and Allied wartime maps and documents.
2. Most positions were wired in and at least partly surrounded by real and/or dummy minefields.
3. 'Armament' in table above refers to larger guns only. Most positions also included machine guns, mortars and other weapons for local defence. Individual casemates and trenches are not shown. In some cases, sources disagree about the precise armament of positions.

la Groin

les Essarts de Langrune

les les de Bernières

Roches

5/736

Mouillage de la Porte

es-sur Mer

la Rive

Dyke

ur-Mer

St. Aubin-sur-Mer

Dyke

Langrune sur-Mer

Halt

9/736

Ston

22

II/736

8/736

Tailleville

Petit En

su

12/736

la Délivrande

Old Mill

DOUVRES
la Délivrande

Ston Halt

8/53

committed without OKW agreement. Hitler wanted to be sure that the landings when they came were not just a diversion to cover other landings elsewhere. He did not want to move too quickly lest he be deceived as to the location of the main blow.

The result of Hitler's directives left 21st Panzer Division, commanded by *Generalmajor* (GenMaj) Edgar Feuchtinger, garrisoned around Caen, ready to attack towards the Normandy coast a few kilometres away. The nearest other armoured reserves, 12th SS Panzer Division *Hitlerjugend* (Hitler Youth) near Lisieux and Panzer Lehr Division around Chartres, were at least a day's march away from the site of the landings.

CHAPTER 3

THE LANDINGS

3rd Canadian Infantry Division carried out its assault over Juno Beach on D-Day as part of I British Corps' attack. Maj-Gen Keller was ordered to land his division in the Mike and Nan sectors and to seize a lodgement stretching 16 km inland to include the high ground to the west of Caen astride the

German infantry on the march with horse-drawn transport. The static 716th Infantry Division had little motor transport of its own and relied heavily on horses and carts to deliver supplies and transport stores. *(NAC PA-162305)*

Panzer IV of 12th SS Panzer Division *Hitlerjugend* moving into Normandy prior to the invasion. *(Bundesarchiv 1011/297/1722/23)*

Caen–Bayeux highway. The landing was to be carried out on either side of the mouth of the River Seulles at Courseulles, with 7th Canadian Infantry Brigade Group, commanded by Brigadier H.W. Foster, on the right and 8th Canadian Infantry Brigade Group, under Brigadier K.G. Blackader, on the left.

On 7th Canadian Infantry Brigade's front astride Courseulles, the two assaulting battalions were to land on beaches on either side of the harbour entrance at the mouth of the River Seulles. On the right, B and D Companies, Royal Winnipeg Rifles, with C Company, 1st Canadian Scottish, under command, were to touch down on Mike Red and Green Beaches. On the left, over Nan Green Beach in front of Courseulles, the assault would be made by A and B Companies, Regina Rifles. 1st Hussars' DD tanks would provide armoured support during the assault stage, A Squadron landing with the Winnipeg Rifles and B Squadron leading the Regina Rifles ashore. Further armoured support was available from the special tanks of 79th Armoured Division. Crab flail tanks from B Squadron, 22nd Dragoons, would clear paths through the minefields and AVREs of 26th Assault Squadron, RE, would help deal with the fixed defences and establish exits from the beaches. The 95-mm guns of the Royal Marine

Armoured Support Regiment's Centaur tanks were also available; they would land from LCT(A)s with the leading waves. Artillery support during the run-in to was to be provided by the 105-mm Priest guns of 12th Field Regiment, RCA, west of the mouth of the Seulles, and 13th Field Regiment, RCA, east of the river.

Each assault battalion would have a strongpoint to neutralise before getting off the beach. On Mike Beach the Winnipeg Rifles would face one 75-mm and two 50-mm guns and many machine guns and mortars in WN-31. On Nan Green, the Regina Rifles would have to deal with one 88-mm and two 75-mm guns in the concrete emplacements of WN-29 at Courseulles. The Regina Rifles would also have to capture WN-30 on the southern edge of Courseulles after clearing the town. All these positions were held by troops from 6th Company, 736th Grenadier Regiment.

The landings on Juno Beach began during the early morning of 6 June 1944 with attacks by RAF Bomber Command and the US Eighth Air Force against coastal batteries and defences. This was followed by raids by fighter-bombers and light and medium bombers of the Allied Expeditionary Air Force. Bombardment Force E then took over. The Royal Navy cruiser *Diadem* opened fire on the battery at Bény-sur-Mer at 0552 hours and at 0619 hours the destroyer *Kempenfelt* fired on gun positions inland from Courseulles and Bernières and behind Nan Beach. Then came a programme of 'beach drenching fire' by ten other

The dunes at Graye-sur-Mer at the back of Mike Beach looking towards the landing site of D Company, Winnipeg Rifles. C Company, 1st Canadian Scottish, landed further along to the west. In the foreground is the main exit from the beach, alongside a monument to the liberation. *(Author)*

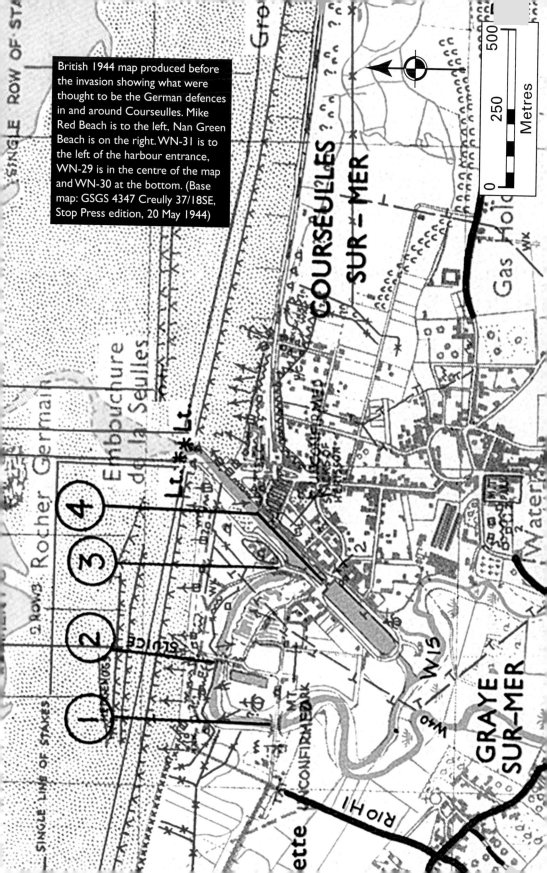

British 1944 map produced before the invasion showing what were thought to be the German defences in and around Courseulles. Mike Red Beach is to the left, Nan Green Beach is on the right. WN-31 is to the left of the harbour entrance, WN-29 is in the centre of the map and WN-30 at the bottom. (Base map: GSGS 4347 Creully 37/18SE, Stop Press edition, 20 May 1944)

Force J Naval Craft Carrying Landings to Juno Beach

Headquarters Ship: HMS *Hilary*   Commodore G.N. Oliver

Assault Group J1: 7th Cdn Inf Bde,   **Mike Red and Green, Nan Green**

Headquarters: Lepe House, Exbury   *Captain A.F. Pugsley*

Assault Group HQ Ship: HMS *Lawford*

Landing Ship Infantry (Large) – LSI(L)

MV *Llangibby Castle*	557th Assault Flotilla	18 Landing Craft Assault (LCA)

Landing Ships Infantry (Medium) – LSI(M)

HMS *Prince Henry*	528th Assault Flotilla	8 LCA
HMS *Queen Emma*	526th Assault Flotilla	8 LCA

Landing Ships Infantry (Hand Hoist) – LSI(H) ex cross-Channel ferries

SS *Canterbury*	509th Assault Flotilla	6 LCA
SS *Duke of Argyll*	517th Assault Flotilla	6 LCA
SS *Invicta*	510th Assault Flotilla	6 LCA
SS *Isle of Thanet*	505th Assault Flotilla	6 LCA
SS *Lairds Isle*	516th Assault Flotilla	6 LCA
SS *Mecklenburg*	511th Assault Flotilla	6 LCA
SS *Ulster Monarch*	521st Assault Flotilla	5 LCA

K Landing Craft Tank Squadron

LCH No. 168

4th Landing Craft Tank Flotilla	12 Landing Craft Tank (LCT)
20th Landing Craft Tank Flotilla	12 LCT
31st Landing Craft Tank Flotilla	12 LCT
102nd Landing Craft Tank Flotilla	12 LCT

destroyers patrolling offshore. This fire was supplemented by the 4.7-inch guns of the gun landing craft (LCG) on either beam of the assault flotilla. These guns continued to fire on enemy strongpoints until the assault craft had touched down.

The troops carrying out the assault were carried over the Channel in liners and ferries converted into infantry landing ships (LSI). These transport vessels anchored off shore and the infantry disembarked into assault landing craft (LCA) to make the final run to the beaches. During the approach, the LCAs were flanked by rocket-firing landing craft (LCT(R)) each capable of pounding the immediate shoreline with over 1,000 5-inch warheads. The noise as the assault craft approached was tremendous.

The two Winnipeg Rifles assault companies and C Company, 1st Canadian Scottish, landed on Mike Red and Green Beaches at around 0750 hours, with all three companies setting down within

1st Support Squadron

333rd Support Flotilla	2 Landing Craft Flak (LCF),
	2 Landing Craft Gun (LCG)
	1 LCT
105th LCT(A) Flotilla	7 LCT (Armoured)
320th LCT (Rocket) Flotilla	8 LCT(R)
900th Support Flotilla	4 LCS(L)
703rd Assault Flotilla	8 LCP(L)

Assault Group J2: 8th Cdn Inf Bde,   **Nan White and Red**
Headquarters: HMS *Squid*, Southampton   *Capt R. J. O. Otway-Ruthven*
Assault Group HQ Ship: HMS *Waveny*

Landing Ships Infantry (Large)

SS *Clan Lamont*	558th Assault Flotilla	17 LCA
SS *Monowai*	544th Assault Flotilla	10 LCA
	556th Assault Flotilla	9 LCA

Landing Ships Infantry (Medium)

HMCS *Prince David*	529th Assault Flotilla	8 LCA

Landing Ships Infantry (Hand Hoist)

HMS *Brigadier*	513th Assault Flotilla	6 LCA
HMS *Duke of Wellington*	506th Assault Flotilla	6 LCA
SS *Isle of Guernsey*	518th Assault Flotilla	6 LCA
SS *Lady of Mann*	512th Assault Flotilla	6 LCA
HMS *St Helier*	515th Assault Flotilla	6 LCA

N Landing Craft Tank Squadron

LCHQ No. 167	
11th Landing Craft Tank Flotilla	12 LCT
22nd Landing Craft Tank Flotilla	12 LCT
30th Landing Craft Tank Flotilla	12 LCT

seven minutes of one another. The DD tanks of A Squadron, 1st Hussars, were late in arriving and did not touch down until about six minutes later. They had been launched closer to shore than originally envisaged, leaving their landing craft 1,500 metres out rather than 7,000 metres as planned, due to the rough nature of the sea. Only ten of the DDs were successfully launched and seven of these reached the shore. Five more landed directly on to the beach from their damaged LCTs. Most of the tanks that 'swam' in stopped in shallow water, dropped their skirts and then opened fire on the defences from there. Their first priority was their own survival and they concentrated their main weapons on the German gun positions, before they could give the infantry effective support by taking on the enemy machine guns.

B Company, Winnipeg Rifles, landed on the left, almost in front of WN-31. The assault craft came under machine-gun, shell and mortar fire while still 700 metres from the beach and this fire continued all the way to the surf. As the men left the landing craft they were confronted with chest-deep water raked by enemy fire and a long 200-metre slog up to the wire at the top of the beach. Each man had to brave his way across this stretch of open sand before there was any chance of cover. To remain near the craft or to lie in the open was to court almost certain death.

Aided by close support fire from the tanks, and with a special kind of determination, the Winnipeg Rifles closed on the barbed-wire entanglements along the 5-metre high dunes and attacked the trenches and pill-boxes. With Bangalore torpedoes they blew gaps in the wire, and with rifles, Sten guns and grenades they swept along the dunes, clearing out the defenders. Some posts gave up swiftly but others had to be cleared by hand-to-hand fighting. The tanks silenced the gun casemates and allowed B Company to cross over the dunes to the bridge across the River Seulles at the rear. The bridge was captured intact, Captain Philip Gower then leading the survivors of the company over the river and on to the 'island' between the Seulles and the harbour that contained the western section of Courseulles. With the company commander were just 26 of the 95 men who had stormed ashore.

Over to the right, on the eastern edge of Mike Green Beach, D Company had landed abreast of B Company. It was further away from the strongpoint and evaded the worst of its fire. Its men were quickly up the beach, through the wire and across the dunes, sweeping through the scattered German positions, firing as they went. They moved through the inundated ground to the rear of the shoreline and crossed the extensive minefield at la Vallette into the village of Graye-sur-Mer, clearing it with little difficulty. Opposition to their move was sporadic, with most of the mortar and artillery fire still being aimed at the beach.

Further to the west, C Company, 1st Canadian Scottish, landed against only slight opposition. The infantry quickly closed on their first objective, the 75-mm casemated gun to their right, only to find that the Royal Navy had already eliminated the weapon with accurate fire. The emplacement was on a slight promontory and a warship far out to sea had managed to get several shells into its more vulnerable sides to blow the casemate apart. Their first job done, the troops of 1st Canadian Scottish swiftly moved on inland to clear the minefields and machine guns around the village of Vaux and its château.

Aerial view of Mike Red Beach to the west of Courseulles, taken in the early afternoon of D-Day. The exit on the left leads inland to Graye-sur-Mer, with the road to Ste-Croix leaving the rear of the village out to the right. The centre and the right of the beach is Mike Green sector, the landing place of D Company, Winnipeg Rifles, and C Company, 1st Canadian Scottish. *(IWM CL27)*

Weapons position guarding the small bridge across the River Seulles behind Mike Red Beach. The bridge connected the beach to the 'island' on the western edge of Courseulles that was formed by a large loop in the river and the harbour. *(Author)*

Two of the DD Shermans of A Squadron, 1st Hussars, which landed with the assault waves were knocked out on the beach by anti-tank fire. The remaining 10 spent the next 30 minutes cruising up and down the shoreline assisting the infantry in the destruction of the defences. However, when the men of the Winnipeg Rifles began their move inland, the tanks were unable to accompany them as there were no exits from the beach ready for them. The specialised armour required to perform this task was late in arriving, eventually turning up 30 minutes after the first waves of infantry. Finally, three Crab tanks managed to flail a path over the dunes and tried to create an exit towards the road to Graye-sur-Mer. Two of them were knocked out by mines. The third bogged down 150 metres along the track, in a deep crater caused by a broken culvert that had filled with water. An AVRE with a fascine came forward to fill the gap but also sank into the crater and blocked the route. A second AVRE placed another fascine into the smashed culvert, which enabled a bridging tank to move forward to lay a box-girder bridge on the top of the submerged tank, resting it on the first AVRE's turret. The hastily laid bridge allowed another Crab to continue flailing a route inland to the lateral road. The exit from the beach was opened for other armour at about 0920 hours. This route over the submerged Churchill AVRE remained open for three hours until the bridge shifted and collapsed into the culvert. Engineers then bulldozed rubble into the hole, burying the tank completely, and established a permanent road off the beach.

Lt Jack Beveridge, wounded by a mine, being brought aboard HMCS *Prince David* from an assault landing craft off Bernières. (*Donovan B. Thorndick, NAC PA-131500*)

Twenty minutes behind the assault came the reserve companies and battalion headquarters. They arrived over beaches still swept with fire, but pressed on through the mêlée and struck out inland. Both companies passed through Graye-sur-Mer, then A Company headed south-west towards Ste-Croix-sur-Mer and C Company advanced and took Banville. The reserve battalion landed next at around 0830 hours. The 1st Canadian Scottish arrived on Mike Beach and found that most of the opposition was from mortar fire from the high ground behind Graye. Some delay was met crossing the minefields around la Vallette, but by 0930 hours the battalion had picked up its C Company and begun its advance across the open cornfields towards Ste-Croix. By this time the artillery had also arrived and was engaging enemy positions inland from the beach. By 1000 hours Brigadier Foster could feel well pleased with 7th Canadian Infantry Brigade's landing on Mike Beach: he had two battalions ashore, the coast defences had been eliminated and troops and armour were already 3 km inland.

A few hundred metres away on the other side of the harbour entrance at Courseulles, 7th Canadian Infantry Brigade's third battalion, the Regina Rifles, had also made its landing. It had arrived a little later than the landings on Mike Beach with A Company touching down at 0809 hours and B Company at around 0815 hours. They were greeted on the sands by the DD tanks of B Squadron, 1st Hussars, which had landed at 0758. All of the squadron's 19 tanks had been successfully launched 4,000 metres out and began swimming ashore in good order; 14 made it to the beach at Courseulles, 1 landed on the wrong beach and 4 'drowned' on the way in. Immediately after the Shermans got ashore they began pounding the concrete emplacements that dominated the landing site, none of which had been damaged by the naval and air bombardment. These large bunkers were sited to fire along the beach, and concrete walls obscured their seaward sides, limiting their field of vision. This enabled some of the tanks to close on them from out of the surf and fire high explosive at an angle through their apertures. It required steady nerves by the tank crews and a high degree of accuracy, but eventually all three of the large emplacements were knocked out.

Nan Green Beach seen from the position of the present-day swimming pool, on the edge of what was strongpoint WN-29. The 75-mm gun casemate was slightly to the left of the picture near the anti-tank ditch and railway line running parallel to the shore. *(Author)*

The presence of tanks already on the beach gave great heart to the Regina Rifles assault companies as their LCAs arrived in a storm of German small arms fire. A Company landed on the right, in front of the main weapons of WN-29, and B Company touched down on the left, to the east of the main resistance. Most of the casualties were taken during the arrival and as the troops closed on the enemy positions across the open expanse of wet

Landing point of A Company, Regina Rifles, on Nan Green Beach at Courseulles. The large 88-mm gun casemate was located where the *Bar de la Mer* now stands at the top of the beach on the right. *(Author)*

sand. A Company veered to the left and got into the machine-gun posts, trenches and wire to begin their sweep along the beach defences. Tank support helped a great deal and German resistance gradually began to slacken. To the east, B Company gained the top of the shore with few casualties. Its men were able to get through the wire and on to the Caen–Douvres–Courselles railway line, which ran behind the beach, fairly quickly, the shock of their attack carrying them through the first line of defence which ran beside the railway line. Behind the beach B Company crossed the anti-tank ditch and entered the town.

The Regina Rifles had divided Courseulles into blocks for each company to clear. B Company now started clearing those parts it had been assigned to sweep while A Company struggled with WN-29 behind it. At 0835 hours the follow-up companies began to arrive. C Company landed and moved into the town and began clearing its blocks without difficulty, but D Company, arriving late at 0855 hours, met disaster. Several of its craft were blown up on obstacles that had been covered by the incoming tide. Only 49 men made it to the beach. By this time, A Company had cleared the beach-front strongpoint and moved into Courseulles, only to be pulled back a little later to clear the fortifications once more after some of the defenders had filtered back through tunnels and trenches into the position.

The specialised armoured support on Nan Green Beach also

arrived late, well behind the assaulting infantry and DD tanks. The Crab flail tanks of B Squadron, 22nd Dragoons, and the AVREs of 26th Assault Squadron, RE, landed slightly east of their planned position but clear of the strongpoint. Two teams of flails beat paths up through the dunes at the top of the beach and across the railway line to the anti-tank ditch. Crossings were then made by AVREs laying fascines into the deep trench and two exits were opened from the beach. At 0900 hours, tanks were moving into the town to join up with the Canadian infantry.

Assault landing craft from HMCS *Prince David* and SS *Monowai* during their run-in to Nan White Beach on D-Day. *(Donovan B. Thorndick, NAC PA-129058)*

During the morning, the Regina Rifles continued with one of the most difficult tasks of the invasion. After carrying out its assault landing, the battalion now had to move into a phase of street fighting and building clearance. The training the battalion had undergone in the bombed-out streets of Southampton was now put to good effect. For the whole morning the four Regina Rifles companies methodically swept their way along the closely-knit streets, gardens and houses of Courseulles, working up through the town towards the château on its southern edge. Just behind the château was another strongpoint, WN-30, consisting of wired positions, machine guns, mortars and minefields. This proved to be stronger on paper than in effect, for the Canadians, aided by tanks, quickly cleared the area with few casualties. Nonetheless, it was early afternoon before the Regina Rifles were able to free themselves from the built-up area and move out towards the next inland objective, the village of Reviers. With troops south of Courseulles and the villages of Vaux and Graye-sur-Mer taken, 7th Canadian Infantry Brigade was now in control of its first phase line Yew. The landings had begun well.

On 8th Canadian Infantry Brigade's front at Bernières, the two-battalion assault was to be made by the Queen's Own Rifles landing on Nan White Beach on the right and the North Shore Regiment on the left on Nan Red Beach. The DD tanks of the Fort Garry Horse would provide support during the assault stage, with B Squadron assisting the Queen's Own Rifles and C Squadron with the North Shore Regiment. Further armoured support was provided by the Crabs from B Squadron, 22nd Dragoons, and the AVREs of 80th Assault Squadron, RE, which were to come ashore with the leading troops.

Nan White Beach today. Prominent in the centre-right of the picture is the large Norman house by the main exit from the beach. B Company, Queen's Own Rifles, landed opposite the strongpoint at the top of the beach, in the mid-left of the picture. *(Author)*

Each battalion would have a strongpoint to neutralise before advancing inland. The Queen's Own Rifles would have to capture WN-28, right in front of Bernières, and the North Shore Regiment would need to eliminate WN-27 at St-Aubin. Both of these positions, which were held by 5th Company, 736th Grenadier Regiment, were sited to bring anti-tank, machine-gun and mortar fire along the landing beaches. Their early capture was the most important task facing each of the assault battalions.

As on 7th Canadian Infantry Brigade's beaches, 8th Canadian Infantry Brigade's assault waves approached their landings later

Strongpoint WN-27 at St-Aubin. Nan Red Beach is around 500 metres behind the strongpoint to the west. The extra height gained from being positioned on the top of a sandy cliff allowed its guns to rake the beach with accurate fire. *(Author)*

than originally planned. The 15-minute delay to H-Hour ordered for both Canadian brigades became more like 20 minutes for the craft approaching the shore at Bernières. Enemy fire during the run-in was light as most of the German artillery in field emplacements inland concentrated their fire on the ships of Force J further out to sea. The larger guns in the beach defences were sited to fire along the shore so that most of the opposition aimed at the assault craft before they touched down was from mortars and machine guns. The state of the sea and the stiff wind that was blowing disrupted the plan to launch the DD tanks, as it had on 7th Canadian Infantry Brigade's front. The senior officer of the LCTs carrying the tanks decided it was too rough to launch them at the designated point and continued towards the shore with them still on board. As a consequence they exited the landing craft much closer to the beach. The tanks raised their DD equipment and engaged their propellers, but really performed what the official history called a 'wet wade', landing behind the assaulting infantry rather than in front of them. This did give them the advantage of being able to steer round the obstacles with their tracks, rather than using the less responsive propellers of the DD equipment. The delays meant that the first craft to arrive on Nan Beach were the LCTs carrying the AVREs of 80th Assault Squadron which touched down just before the infantry.

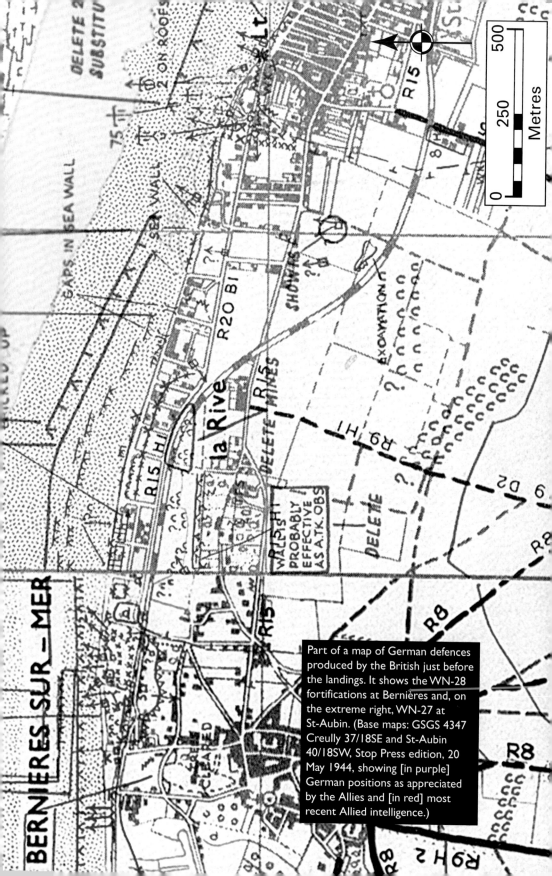

Part of a map of German defences produced by the British just before the landings. It shows the WN-28 fortifications at Bernières and, on the extreme right, WN-27 at St-Aubin. (Base maps: GSGS 4347 Creully 37/18SE and St-Aubin 40/18SW, Stop Press edition, 20 May 1944, showing [in purple] German positions as appreciated by the Allies and [in red] most recent Allied intelligence.)

Several emplacements once forming part of WN-28 remain today. B Company, Queen's Own Rifles, lost 65 men trying to take the fortifications. *(Author)*

At 0810 hours both assault formations of infantry hit Nan White and Red Beaches. The leading Queen's Own Rifles companies had a mixed reception. B Company ran straight into difficulties when it landed 200 metres east of its correct position, right in front of the Bernières strongpoint. Within the first few minutes a great number of casualties were taken. Determined action by Lieutenant Herbert and a few of his men allowed them to close on the machine-gun post that was doing most of the destruction and silence it with grenades and Sten guns. This action allowed more of the company to approach the rest of WN-28's concrete defences and deal with them. Many more men were killed and injured before the infantry got amongst the fortifications and it took a considerable amount of time to clear the maze of trenches and pill-boxes that made up the site. A well-established mortar post set in a concrete emplacement right on the sea wall did a great amount of damage. Tank support from B Squadron, Fort Garry Horse, was sporadic, as the tanks landed after the leading waves and took some time to become effective. By the time the tanks' 75-mm guns were firing at the pill-boxes, B Company had already taken 65 casualties. The Fort Garry Horse's own war diary records that the Queen's Own Rifles suffered severely before B Squadron could intervene.

On the right of the attack, A Company fared a little better. Its troops braved the small arms fire that swept the beach and quickly got amongst the wire at the top amongst the sand dunes. Delay was fatal; there was no shelter to be had in the surf and the only means of survival was to get off the beach as quickly as possible. At the top of the beach the leading waves became engaged in some hand-to-hand fighting with the defenders dug in along the dunes. A few local resistance nests were quickly cleared and the bulk of the company was able to press on inland. Most resistance came at the back of the beach from mortar fire as they moved across the open ground to the west of Bernières. Minefields also slowed A Company's progress and machine-gun fire forced many to take cover amongst the dips in the dunes and clumps of rough grass. Groups of Germans in houses on the western side of the village kept the Canadians pinned down and remained a problem until the follow-up companies got off the beach and swept through the built-up area of Bernières.

Behind the leading waves the remaining Queen's Own Rifles companies landed through the rolling surf, which was still being driven up the beach by the incoming tide. Many of the submerged German obstacles found targets among the flat-

DD tank of the Fort Garry Horse moving along the road from the centre of St-Aubin up to the seafront strongpoint. The tank is supporting B Company, North Shore Regiment, during its attack on WN-27. *(IWM B5227)*

Section of Nan White Beach looking eastwards from strongpoint WN-28 towards Nan Red Beach. B Company, Queen's Own Rifles, landed at this point as did the specialised armour of No. 2 Team, 80th Assault Squadron, RE. The portion of the sea wall between the two concrete emplacements is of 1944 vintage. (Author)

bottomed assault craft, snaring them on jagged spikes or blowing them apart with underwater mines. C and D Companies suffered heavy casualties to their craft as they came in. Once ashore, these troops were able to move up the beach and get over the high sea wall and across the railway line running behind the seafront. The men of B Company, who were still raking the enemy position with close quarters fire, diverted the attention of the German defenders in the strongpoint away from C and D Companies. Twenty minutes after the first assault had hit the beach, the Canadians were starting to clear Bernières.

Landing with the leading waves were the tanks of B Squadron, 22nd Dragoons, and 80th Assault Squadron, RE. They arrived in their LCTs and began the task of clearing paths through the minefields and establishing exits. No. 1 Team landed as planned directly opposite its proposed gap. A Crab tank flailed up to the sea wall followed by an AVRE which dropped its bridge right on target but the first AVRE that ground its way up the ramp hit a mine and blocked it. An armoured bulldozer came forward and pushed the AVRE aside, but set off another mine, killing the driver. There was then a pause while the lane was cleared by hand. Two more Crabs then crossed the bridge and continued flailing through the minefield to the road and railway behind the beach, then turned eastwards and flailed a path to the second exit that was being built on the left side of the Bernières beach.

This second exit was actually being constructed 200 metres east of its target because of enemy fire. The LCTs carrying No. 2 Team had landed further to the east than planned and came under immediate fire from the 50-mm gun in WN-28. Two of the leading AVREs were hit, including the one carrying the bridge to gap the sea wall. A Crab cleared a path to the wall and found a blocked ramp. AVREs came forward and blasted a path through the obstruction with their petard mortars allowing an exit to be cleared by the supporting engineers. In less than an hour, two exits had been made off the beach and were open for traffic.

The former railway station at Bernières. The rail line is long gone and the building is now a tourist office. To the left is the main exit from the beach. *(Author)*

Away to the east, between Bernières and St-Aubin, the North Shore Regiment attacked Nan Red Beach with two companies. A Company landed on the right and had the task of sweeping the Germans from the eastern edge of Bernières. It landed and got amongst the buildings with few casualties, but lost many more men from snipers and mines as they tried to clear the buildings along the seafront. Nonetheless, progress was steady and a link-up was soon made with the Queen's Own Rifles.

To the left, B Company, North Shore Regiment, had been given the objective of silencing strongpoint WN-27 at St-Aubin. This position dominated the shore along Nan Red Beach and the

HISTORY

seaward side of St-Aubin itself. The strongpoint was very active as the assault waves approached the beach, its larger guns aiming at the tank landing craft and its machine guns and mortars sweeping the lighter assault vessels. The guns knocked out several of the DD tanks and AVREs as soon as they hit the beach, but it was the lighter weapons that caused so much damage to the Canadian infantry. Fire from within the fortifications and from along the sandy cliffs swept through the men of the North Shore Regiment as they left the LCAs and they began dropping all along the beach. All of the infantrymen who were able to now made the dash across 100 metres of open sand towards the sea wall at the top of the beach and the shelter of the low cliffs beneath the seaside villas. Here they were protected from frontal fire but were still exposed to fire along the shore from the strongpoint. Safety lay off the beach and everyone knew it.

Nan Red Beach, looking towards St-Aubin. B Company, North Shore Regiment, landed here and the large house in the centre is opposite the landing place of 48 RM Commando. The whole beach was raked by fire from the strongpoint at St-Aubin, located behind the slight headland in the left-centre. *(Author)*

Bangalore torpedoes were placed in the wire and paths blown through the obstacles. More explosives cleared routes through minefields and the men of B Company, North Shore Regiment, struggled free and on to the lateral road at the rear. Here they reorganised themselves and set about attacking the strongpoint from the town side. The way forward, however, was blocked with more wire, mines and pill-boxes. Tank support eventually arrived and the advance inched forward slowly. Inside the

The sea wall on Nan Red Beach after the assault. This picture was taken at high tide during the late morning when the width of the beach had been reduced to just a few metres. *(IWM B5225)*

fortification, undaunted by the Allied troops and tanks closing in around them, the strongpoint's garrison continued to bring devastating fire down along the length of Nan Red Beach.

Following behind the assault companies, C and D Companies, North Shore Regiment, now began to land. They set down a little west of B Company's landing place and evaded the worst of the fire. They were reasonably quickly off the beach and began their moves to secure the southern end of St-Aubin, preparatory to the advance inland on Tailleville and the radar station at Douvres.

Behind them the specialised armour had landed on Nan Red and was setting about its tasks. No. 3 Team successfully laid a bridge across the sea wall and created an exit, but No. 4 Team landed closer to the St-Aubin strongpoint and ran into difficulties. It lost its AVRE bridge tank through a collision and snipers killed several tank crewmen. The flails turned westwards away from the fire and flailed along the beach to create a gap nearer to No. 3 Team's exit. No vehicle exit was made on the eastern end of Nan Red Beach until later that morning.

The Régiment de la Chaudière, 8th Canadian Infantry Brigade's reserve battalion, began to land on Nan White Beach at about 0830 hours. Its landing craft had a difficult passage

German prisoners under guard by the sea wall between the Norman house and strongpoint WN-28 at Bernières. *(Frank L. Dubervill, NAC PA-133754)*

through the beach obstacles as the incoming tide had covered most of them. A Company had a particularly bad experience when its boats struck a thick concentration of steel obstacles and were hit by accurate mortar fire at the same time, causing most of the craft to founder before touching down. Many of the troops discarded their equipment and swam for the shore. Just one of the eight assault boats launched from the landing ship *Prince David* made the beach undamaged. Although disrupted in their passage, most of the men reached the shore safely and joined the mêlée of troops sheltering behind the sea wall, seeking cover while the Queen's Own Rifles dealt with the strongpoint.

With the beach defences well and truly pierced, the three battalions now began moving inland, although there was still a great deal of German resistance actively hindering the landings. Even though the Queen's Own Rifles and North Shore Regiment had not cleared their respective strongpoints, there were sufficient troops ashore to begin clearing the areas behind them.

More infantry, tanks, transport and equipment started to arrive as 9th Canadian Infantry Brigade now began to make its landings. This coincided with the approach of high tide and the beach was reduced to a strip of sand just a few metres wide. The few exits that were open could not cope with the traffic and many of the routes into and through Bernières were still blocked by anti-tank ditches and enemy positions. Not surprisingly the great press of men and machines closing inexorably on the beach reduced the shoreline to a chaotic mass of jammed vehicles and armour. It took some time to sort out the mess, causing the initial expansion of the beachhead to fall behind schedule.

Over to the east, landing behind the North Shore Regiment on Nan Red Beach were the Royal Marines of 48 Commando. They touched down into heavy and accurate fire from the strongpoint at St-Aubin. They also had the misfortune of having three of their six LCI(S)s strike underwater obstacles near the beach. One craft, carrying Lieutenant-Colonel (Lt-Col) J.L. Moulton's headquarters, shrugged itself free, but the other two unfortunate vessels became anchored beneath the fire of WN-27. The commandos on board tried to swim for shore, but most of those who attempted this were swept away to their deaths. Those aboard Z Troop's craft were taken off by a passing LCT and an LCA, but most of Y Troop's men were trans-shipped to another LCT which promptly took them back to England, despite their protests.

The landings made by 48 RM Commando quickly became a complete shambles. The North Shore Regiment had not secured the beach and it was still swept by accurate small arms fire and shelled by German artillery. Casualties were severe; by the time Moulton had rallied his men at their rendezvous point, only around 60 per cent of them remained. Before the day was out, 48 Commando had lost almost half of its strength including five of its six troop commanders.

48 Commando's objectives were to clear the eastern side of St-Aubin and the next village of Langrune-sur-Mer, then eliminate the seafront strongpoint WN-26. It was then to link up with 41 RM Commando, which was to advance east from Sword Beach, thus linking the British and Canadian beaches. Lt-Col Moulton's commandos made the advance to Langrune and attacked the strongpoint, but they were too lightly armed to overcome its massive fortifications. Two Centaur tanks from 2nd Royal Marine Armoured Support Regiment came forward to help, only to run foul of mines whist bombarding a thick concrete wall that barred the way into WN-26. By early evening it was clear that the attack had stalled. Intelligence then received at 4th Special Service Brigade HQ warned of a possible counter-

Troops of the North Nova Scotia Highlanders and Highland Light Infantry of Canada landing over Nan White Beach on D-Day. The picture was taken to the east of Bernières at high tide. The smoke in the background is from burning buildings in Courseulles, 2 km to the west. *(Gilbert A. Milne, NAC PA-116533)*

Wounded infantry await evacuation at a casualty clearing station on the top of Nan White Beach at Bernières. The 50-mm casemated gun of strongpoint WN-28 can be seen in the background. *(Frank L. Dubervill, NAC PA-133971)*

attack by panzer forces. 48 RM Commando was therefore told to hold the perimeter and prepare a defensive cordon around Langrune, so as to anchor the left flank of the Juno landings. Its proposed link-up with troops from Sword Beach never took place, for 41 RM Commando was held at another strongpoint at Lion-sur-Mer on the edge of Sword Beach 3 km away.

CHAPTER 4

THE DRIVE INLAND

By late morning on 6 June it was clear that 3rd Canadian Infantry Division's assault landings on Juno Beach had been successful. The outer crust of the Atlantic Wall defences had been broken and troops were pressing inland against only light opposition. The initial phase line Yew, 2 km from the sea along the line from Vaux to St-Aubin, had been reached by mid-morning. Maj-Gen Keller had two of his three infantry brigades off the beaches and their tank support was beginning to fan out to back them up. Artillery, transport, supplies and the follow-up brigade were now coming ashore – albeit slowly over narrow and congested beaches – allowing the division to press on with the next part of the operation. The advance to phase line Elm, an arc of villages 9 km inland where the Canadians would organise a fortress line to consolidate the beachhead, now began. Once 9th Canadian Infantry Brigade had completed its landings and reached this phase line, the final push to the D-Day objective Oak would begin. Keller and his corps commander, Lt-Gen Crocker, could be mildly satisfied with the way the day was progressing.

Some 15 km away to the south-east, in his bunker in a quarry at la Folie, the commander of German 716th Infantry Division, GenLt Richter, was not so pleased with events. Since the early hours his men had been forced to contend with the parachute landings made by 6th British Airborne Division on the eastern side of the River Orne. Then, at 0725 hours, 3rd British Infantry Division had landed on Sword Beach. Simultaneously 50th (Northumbrian) Division had stormed ashore over Gold Beach. Finally, at around 0800 hours, the Canadians had landed in the centre around Courseulles. Four Allied divisions had descended on the sector defended by his men and his division was being smashed to pieces by the onslaught. There were no immediate reserves to help, for those units of the nearby 21st Panzer Division that were to hand had already been committed against the parachute landings – and were experiencing scant success against the airborne bridgehead. The rest of the panzer division was trying to make progress towards the landings along roads swept by Allied fighter-bombers.

Defending the Juno Beach sector opposite the Canadians was 2nd Battalion of *Oberst* (Colonel) Ludwig Krug's 736th Grenadier Regiment (II/736th). Krug had his regimental command post just to the south of Colleville in an underground complex known to the British as 'Hillman'. II/736th was commanded by *Hauptmann* (Captain) Deptolla from his headquarters in the château at Tailleville, some 3 km south of St-Aubin. Deptolla had just two companies of infantry defending Juno Beach: 5th Company at Bernières and St-Aubin, and 6th Company at Courseulles and along Mike Beach around WN-31

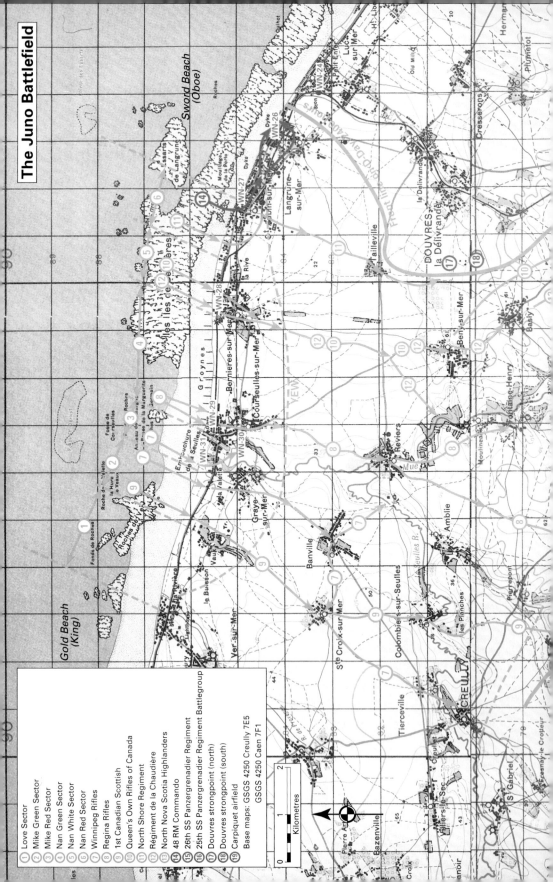

The Juno Battlefield

①	Love Sector
②	Mike Green Sector
③	Mike Red Sector
④	Nan Green Sector
⑤	Nan White Sector
⑥	Nan Red Sector
⑦	Winnipeg Rifles
⑧	Regina Rifles
⑨	1st Canadian Scottish
⑩	Queen's Own Rifles of Canada
⑪	North Shore Regiment
⑫	Régiment de la Chaudière
⑬	North Nova Scotia Highlanders
⑭	48 RM Commando
⑮	26th SS Panzergrenadier Regiment
⑯	25th SS Panzergrenadier Regiment Battlegroup
⑰	Douvres strongpoint (north)
⑱	Douvres strongpoint (south)
⑲	Carpiquet airfield

Base maps: GSGS 4250 Creully 7E5
GSGS 4250 Caen 7F1

Gold Beach (King)

Sword Beach (Oboe)

Kilometres

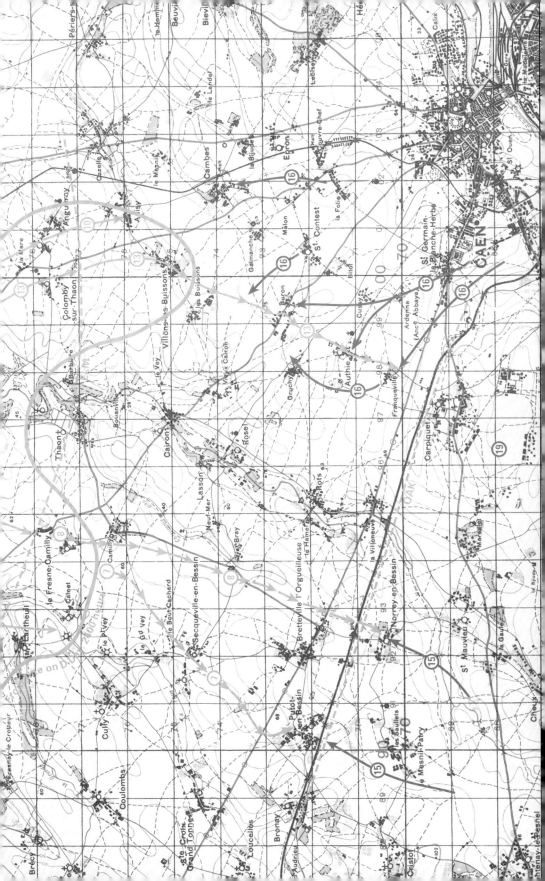

(possibly plus part of 7th Company near WN-31). In addition 8th Company (8/736th) was near the II/736th HQ. There were also elements of 726th Grenadier Regiment to the west of Courseulles and its 2nd Battalion (II/726th), led by *Major* Lehmann, had its HQ just behind Graye-sur-Mer in Ste-Croix.

To bolster these troops, Richter had the dubious services of 441st *Ost* Battalion. The battalion was inserted in the line to the west of Courseulles behind Mike Beach and into the sector covered by Gold Beach. It was suspected that the Russian battalion would be of little use when called upon to fight and this was borne out by events. Richter commented that, when the Canadians came into contact with one of its companies near Vaux, 'Its troops all ran away from the battle with the exception of a few German officers and NCOs.'

German prisoners under guard on Nan White Beach at Bernières on D-Day. The troops with a white band around their helmets and a white circular patch on their sleeves are British beach group personnel, probably from 5th Royal Berkshires. The picture was taken in front of the 50-mm gun emplacement on the sea wall within strongpoint WN-28. *(Frank L. Dubervill, NAC PA-136280)*

The vaunted Atlantic Wall, impregnable against an Allied seaborne attack, or so the Führer believed, was in fact only half completed and was manned by second-rate troops and foreign conscripts. 3rd Canadian Infantry Division had sliced its way through it along Juno Beach with greater ease and with fewer casualties than had been anticipated. Once through the fortifications along the shoreline there was little inland to stop a rapid expansion of the beachhead. Richter admitted after the war that his sector had been too thinly defended. His troops were 'strung out like a string of pearls', unable to withstand the weight of Allied power that was thrown against them. Once the companies along the seafront had been swept aside and 441st *Ost* Battalion had melted away into the hinterland, the way seemed open for a Canadian drive to the outskirts of Caen. If Rommel had had his way, this would have been the moment that an armoured counter-attack would have been launched against the landings. But, at that moment, Rommel was in Germany visiting his wife and not directing the battle.

At 1050 hours Maj-Gen Keller ordered 9th Canadian Infantry Brigade to land over Nan White Beach at Bernières. It had been planned for the brigade to use both Nan Red and White Beaches to get ashore, but the continued resistance from the strongpoint at St-Aubin meant that Nan Red Beach was still under too much fire and had been temporarily closed. As a result, the whole brigade had to land through Bernières and make its way southwards to Bény-sur-Mer over the one available road. This led to vast traffic jams and a slow build-up, delaying the brigade's move towards its assembly area. It was 1140 hours before the first battalion, the North Nova Scotia Highlanders, began its landing and its men and vehicles immediately became bogged down on the beaches and in the crowded narrow streets of Bernières. Landing with the North Nova Scotia Highlanders were the tanks of 2nd Canadian Armoured Brigade's follow-up regiment, 27th Canadian Armoured Regiment (The Sherbrooke Fusiliers). Congestion caused all movement to slow almost to a halt. The most important men on Nan White Beach that morning were the military police and beach groups acting as traffic regulators. It was early afternoon before 9th Canadian Infantry Brigade's next two infantry battalions began to arrive and they too descended on to a congested beach with clogged exits. The good start made by the division was beginning to be lost to administrative and logistical problems of alarming proportions.

Elsewhere, 7th and 8th Canadian Infantry Brigades' assault and follow-up battalions were pressing inland. On the right, from Mike Beach, the 1st Canadian Scottish had taken back its C Company from the Winnipeg Rifles and had advanced on Ste-Croix. Here one company was involved in the protracted task of capturing the village and reducing *Major* Lehmann's II/726th

Nan White Beach at Bernières late in the morning of 6 June, showing the sector assaulted by B Company, Queen's Own Rifles. Strongpoint WN-28 can be seen in the centre left of the picture where the beach curves towards the sea. The main exit from the beach and the Norman house are on the right of the picture. *(US National Archives)*

headquarters. The remainder of 1st Canadian Scottish were advancing towards the villages of Colombiers-sur-Seulles and Pierrepont. The Winnipeg Rifles had moved off through Graye-sur-Mer, passed through Banville, and were making for Creully to link up with 7th Battalion, the Green Howards, from 50th (Northumbrian) Division, who had landed over Gold Beach. Progress was good against light and sporadic resistance. The Regina Rifles had broken free of Courseulles by early afternoon and had captured Reviers and the important Pont de Reviers across the River Seulles to the west of the village. Supporting tanks from B Squadron, 1st Hussars, assisted with the move, but the squadron had five Shermans knocked out on the high ground to the south of the bridge by an 88-mm anti-tank gun before the offending weapon could be destroyed. With tanks up with the leading troops of the brigade, hopes were high of continuing with the moves inland according to the timetable laid down at the start of the operation.

8th Canadian Infantry Brigade's three battalions were having mixed fortunes in their moves inland from Nan Beach. The Queen's Own Rifles were still clearing the area around Bernières of pockets of the enemy and trying to establish a firm base from which operations inland were to develop. The Régiment de la Chaudière was making slow progress towards Bény-sur-Mer over the open plateau behind Bernières, experiencing difficulties from two 88-mm anti-tank guns that had good observation across the open ground. On its way to Bény the battalion detached a company to capture the 100-mm gun battery to the west of the village, which had been firing on the beach. The Régiment de la Chaudière eventually reached Bény and cleared the village during the mid-afternoon, then pushed on towards Basly and Colomby-sur-Thaon to reach phase line Elm. By early evening both 7th and 8th Canadian Infantry Brigades were on this intermediate phase line and the way was clear for 9th Brigade and the armour to push on to phase line Oak along the Caen–Bayeux railway line.

On the extreme left, the North Shore Regiment took all morning to subdue strongpoint WN-27 and clear St-Aubin before it could start out towards the village of Tailleville, 3 km to the south. Here the battalion was shocked to find that the village, containing II/736th's battalion headquarters, had been made into a fortress, with the château and grounds on its northern outskirts converted into a strongpoint of tunnels, trenches, minefields and

HISTORY

pill-boxes. It took the whole day to clear the area and it was almost nightfall before the battalion had consolidated a defensive position around the village, too late to put in an attack on the radar station at Douvres-la-Délivrande. Things were beginning to fall behind schedule for Maj-Gen Keller's division.

Pill-box by the château wall at Tailleville. This was part of the defences protecting the headquarters of II/736th Grenadier Regiment, and was attacked from the left by the North Shore Regiment during the afternoon of D-Day. *(Author)*

By late afternoon the first of 9th Canadian Infantry Brigade's battalions, the North Nova Scotia Highlanders, had extricated itself from the chaos near the beach and made it to an assembly area near Bény-sur-Mer. At 1820 hours it pushed through the Régiment de la Chaudière at Basly and Colomby with its infantry riding on the backs of Sherbrooke Fusiliers tanks and became the advance guard of the Canadian landings. The North Nova Scotia Highlanders moved on through phase line Elm towards Villons-les-Buissons. Some resistance had been met in Colomby and more was experienced near Villons, forcing the infantry to dismount and put in set-piece attacks. The resistance was slight, but it was enough to slow the advance considerably. Further movement south now became cautious and measured, for Maj-Gen Keller was becoming concerned with events unfolding on his left flank.

Just a few kilometres to the east, through the gap still open between the Canadians and 3rd British Infantry Division's landings on Sword Beach, 21st Panzer Division had launched an

Crew from 3rd Anti-Tank Regiment, RCA, remove waterproofing from their M10 Wolverine after arriving over Mike Red Beach. *(Ken Bell, NAC PA-132989)*

armoured counter-attack towards the sea late that afternoon. The strength of the German attack was blunted by the tanks and anti-tank guns of 185th (British) Infantry Brigade, but some panzers and accompanying panzergrenadiers actually made it to the coast near Lion-sur-Mer between the two landing zones. Maj-Gen Keller greeted this news with some alarm, for the more he pushed his troops forward, the more exposed his flanks would become to the enemy. The Queen's Own Rifles were brought up on the left through Anguerny to Anisy to steady this eastern side of the lodgement and the North Nova Scotia Highlanders cautiously resumed their advance into Villons-les-Buissons. The moment for bold moves was, however, now past. It was clear that phase line Oak would not be reached before dark and Keller gave orders for the infantry and tanks to 'form a fortress' around Anisy and Villons and dig in for the night.

Late in the afternoon of D-Day, follow-up troops land over Nan White Beach at Bernières and trudge across the wide expanse of sand to the main beach exit near the Norman house. *(Ken Bell, NAC PA-135959)*

Despite its good start, the division had not been able to make the progress it had planned. From the very beginning, starting with the setting back of the times of the landings, delays had continued to build up throughout the day. As the hours passed, the timetable fell further and further behind. The lateness of the landing meant that beach obstacles could not be cleared before the incoming tide swept over them. This resulted in the beaches being choked by damaged craft, further delaying the arrival of follow-up units. The restricted depth of the beach at high tide led to more confusion and congestion. Difficulties opening beach exits compounded these delays until the whole area along Juno Beach became clogged with traffic. German resistance at St-Aubin and Tailleville closed one of the exit roads from Nan Beach and forced both 8th and 9th Canadian Infantry Brigades to use the remaining road south to Bény, further exacerbating traffic problems. Contrary to what planners believed would be the cause

D-DAY Casualties, 3rd Canadian Infantry Division

	Killed	Wounded	Missing
7th Canadian Infantry Brigade – *Assault Brigade*			
Royal Winnipeg Rifles	57	64	5
Regina Rifles	45	61	–
1st Battalion, Canadian Scottish	22	64	–
8th Canadian Infantry Brigade – *Assault Brigade*			
Queen's Own Rifles of Canada	61	77	–
Régiment de la Chaudière	18	37	42
North Shore Regiment	34	88	–
9th Canadian Infantry Brigade – *Follow-up Brigade*			
Stormont, Dundas & Glengarry Highlanders	1	13	–
North Nova Scotia Highlanders	4	5	–
Highland Light Infantry of Canada	–	–	–
Divisional Machine Gun Battalion			
Cameron Highlanders of Ottawa	1	3	–
2nd Canadian Armoured Brigade			
1st Hussars	22	18	–
Fort Garry Horse	14	10	–
Sherbrooke Fusiliers	–	2	–

Other Canadian and British units suffered over 400 casualties in the Juno operation on D-Day.

of a slow expansion of the beachhead, it was not the German opposition that was the biggest problem in the afternoon and evening of D-Day, but the difficulties experienced in getting a highly mechanised army ashore and deployed.

The division spent the night of 6 June establishing itself along the area of intermediate phase line Elm. The front line ran in a ragged arc from around Creully in the west, through Pierrepont, le Fresne-Camilly, Colomby-sur-Thaon, Villons-les-Buissons to Anisy, just about half way towards the division's final objectives on Oak. All were disappointed that the drive inland had not been more successful or pressed home with more urgency. After all, opposition behind the beach was relatively light, especially in front of 7th Canadian Infantry Brigade, and all the battalions had tank support with which to counter their opponents.

This lack of resistance inland was demonstrated by the exploits of Lieutenant Bill McCormick's troop of tanks from C Squadron, 1st Hussars. His Shermans, supporting the Winnipeg Rifles, had got ahead of the infantry in the area of Camilly and just kept on going. McCormick led his tanks south through empty lanes and villages, shooting up parties of infantry and a scout car *en route*.

HISTORY

German prisoners being marched across Nan White Beach out to a tank landing craft to embark for POW camps in Britain. *(Ken Bell, NAC PA-133742)*

They motored on through Bretteville-l'Orgueilleuse, across the Caen–Bayeux road and railway and on towards the airfield at Carpiquet. McCormick stopped in enemy territory 8 km ahead of the nearest friendly infantry, but his advance was not exploited even though he had shown that there was nothing ahead of 7th Canadian Infantry Brigade and the way was open to phase line Oak. McCormick was told to turn back and join his regiment for the night in the area between Pierrepont and Fontaine-Henry. The young lieutenant's exploit was unique in Normandy, for his troop of tanks was the only element of the entire Allied seaborne invasion force to reach the D-Day final objectives!

On either side of 3rd Canadian Infantry Division, the landings over the adjacent beaches had had mixed fortunes. 50th Division had gained its lodgement on Gold Beach and was pushing inland against sporadic opposition. Still short of its final objectives, it did have one armoured and four infantry brigades ashore. On the left of the Canadians, 3rd British Infantry Division had likewise established itself inland from its landings on Sword Beach. Its drive to the important objective of Caen had failed after it had the misfortune to meet 21st Panzer Division's counter-attack head on. A few of GenMaj Feuchtinger's tanks had penetrated to the sea and caused great concern in the Allied camp, but this small force withdrew in the late evening when confronted with the spectacle of a massed airborne drop behind them as the third of 6th British Airborne Division's brigades made its landings around Ranville and St-Aubin-d'Arquenay.

British Second Army was ashore and through the fortifications of the Atlantic Wall, but none of its divisions had achieved their final objectives. The same was true for the Americans landing over Omaha and Utah Beaches. First US Army had seized a lodgement, but was some way behind its timetable for deployment inland. Nonetheless, the achievements of D-Day had to be seen as a spectacular success. The Allies had a foothold on the continent of Europe, the number of casualties was well below what was predicted and reinforcements and supplies were closing inexorably on the beaches to support the drive inland. The next few days would be crucial. The Germans would counter-attack the landings in force with armoured divisions, of that there could be no doubt. The question was, were the forces ashore strong enough to resist them?

CHAPTER 5

D-DAY+1, 7 JUNE

At daylight on 7 June, 3rd Canadian Infantry Division braced itself for the expected dawn counter-attack, but none came. The night had been relatively quiet on the Canadian front, for the Germans were not yet ready to move against the landings. The previous day had seen a flurry of orders and counter-orders within the German High Command as they sought to assemble a powerful force capable of striking against the Allied beachhead. The troops on the spot, from 716th Infantry and 21st Panzer Divisions, were unable to intervene. Richter's 716th Infantry Division had been virtually wiped out and, because of their earlier commitment against the airborne landings, Feuchtinger's tanks were unable to mount a powerful enough attack to cause real damage. The man who might have been able to get things moving sooner, Field Marshal Rommel, was away in Germany visiting his wife on her birthday. Much to his disgust, the day, and the critical moment that he had always stressed was the most important time to move against the landings, had been lost.

During the late afternoon of 6 June, Hitler's OKW staff finally gained his approval to release the armoured reserves. Both 12th SS Panzer Division and Panzer Lehr Division were transferred to the control of Rommel's Army Group B for use by Seventh Army. Initially they were to be attached to General Marck's LXXXIV Corps for immediate deployment, but later that day this order was changed when I SS Panzer Corps was activated under the command of *SS-Gruppenführer* (Lt-Gen) Josef 'Sepp' Dietrich. 12th SS Panzer and Panzer Lehr, together with 21st Panzer and 716th Infantry Divisions, were now to be grouped in Dietrich's I SS Panzer Corps and allocated the sector to the east of LXXXIV Corps, that is the area from Bayeux to Caen. The new corps boundary was to run along the line of 716th Infantry Division's old positions in the west and the River Dives in the east. These moves would eventually bring one infantry and three panzer divisions into the line against 3rd British, 3rd Canadian and 50th Divisions. The Germans were now, at last, massing their armour to drive the Allies back into the sea. Before an attack could begin, however, the panzer divisions would have to be brought into the line over roads dominated by Allied air power; this was no easy task. 12th SS Panzer was over 100 km from the landings and Panzer Lehr more than double that distance away.

12th SS Panzer Division's advanced units began their march to the invasion area on the evening of D-Day, harried by Allied fighter-bombers all of the way. *SS-Standartenführer* (Colonel) Kurt Meyer, commander of 25th SS Panzergrenadier Regiment, pushed on ahead of his men and arrived in Caen late that night to report to GenLt Richter at his command post in his underground bunker at la Folie. There he also met GenMaj Feuchtinger. The two tired generals briefed Meyer on the situation and the setbacks suffered since the landings. Whilst at Richter's HQ, Meyer took a call from his divisional commander, *SS-Brigadeführer* (Maj-Gen) Fritz Witt, telling him that I SS Panzer Corps had ordered an attack for the next day, 7 June. At 1600 hours, 12th SS and 21st Panzer Divisions were to move against the landings. The two units were to advance on either side of the Caen–Luc-sur-Mer railway line and to push the invaders into the sea. Meyer realised that this attack would be impossible to mount at that time with

Field Marshal von Rundstedt and officers of 12th SS Panzer Division inspect the division's reconnaissance troop before D-Day. *(Bundesarchiv 1011/297/1740/09A)*

the full division as most of it was still on the move into the area. Some units were not expected until nightfall the next day. Witt told him to attack regardless. Meyer was ordered to form as much of the division as had arrived into a battlegroup under his command and attack beside 21st Panzer Division as instructed.

Meyer left the meeting a little disappointed by the defeated and tired attitude of Richter and Feuchtinger. He had every confidence that his panzergrenadiers would, as he put it, 'throw the little fish back into the sea'. He established his command post at a café in a suburb of Caen at St-Germain-la-Blanche-Herbe while his staff organised a tactical HQ in the buildings of the medieval abbey of Ardennes, 2 km to the east of la Folie. Throughout the night of 6–7 June, more and more units of the division arrived and were dispersed among the lanes and hedgerows round the abbey, gathering strength for the attack.

At about the same time, 8 km away to the north-west, at 0130 hours on the morning of 7 June, Brigadier Foster called an orders group of his battalion commanders to outline his plans for 7th Canadian Infantry Brigade's continuation of its move inland. The advance was to be resumed at 0600 hours, with the Winnipeg Rifles on the left and the Regina Rifles on the right. 1st Canadian Scottish would advance down the centre.

The northern gatehouse and medieval church of Ardennes abbey seen from the direction of Authie. Kurt Meyer directed the battle against 9th Canadian Infantry Brigade from one of the turrets on the upper right of the building. *(Author)*

The Canadian battalions in the eastern sector of the division's lodgement had received some attention from the Germans during the night. Both the Régiment de la Chaudière and the North Nova Scotia Highlanders had skirmished with small parties from 21st Panzer Division's 192nd Panzergrenadier Regiment, but these local attacks were easily beaten off. Brigadier Cunningham's 9th Canadian Infantry Brigade resumed its march at 0745 hours. An advance guard of North Nova Scotia Highlanders supported by Sherbrooke Fusiliers moved south from Villons-les-Buissons towards Buron, with the light Stuart tanks of the Sherbrooke Fusiliers' reconnaissance troop in the lead. Behind them came C Company, North Nova Scotia Highlanders, riding on the battalion's carriers. Next came a platoon of medium machine guns from the division's machine-gun battalion, the Cameron Highlanders of Ottawa; a troop of tank destroyers from 62nd Anti-Tank Regiment, RCA; two assault sections of pioneers; and four towed 6-pdr guns. Following behind the advance group came the remainder of the North Nova Scotia Highlanders riding on Sherbrooke Fusiliers Sherman tanks.

At first opposition to the Allied move was slight. The leading group moved across the open fields south of Villons-les-Buissons and into Buron. Then resistance began to mount. Two 88-mm guns had to be eliminated before the village could be occupied at around 1140 hours. Mortar fire from St-Contest to the east now started to pour down on the Canadians. The advance continued and infantry pressed on out of Buron towards Authie, while tanks deployed in the open country between the two villages. The tanks opened fire on targets in Authie allowing the advance guard, supported by C Company, to sweep into the village. After a short skirmish Authie was taken and C Company moved further forward to dig in on the southern edge of the village while the tanks pressed on to the hamlet of Franqueville, within sight of Carpiquet airfield. German fire, mainly from mortars and artillery, continued to shower down on the North Nova Scotia Highlanders from the area around St-Contest with gradually increasing intensity. 9th Canadian Infantry Brigade's advance guard was now within 2 km of its D-Day objectives.

Watching this advance from his vantage point in one of the turrets of the medieval abbey at Ardennes, just 1,500 metres to the south-east of Authie, was SS Colonel Kurt Meyer. 9th Canadian Infantry Brigade was, to his amazement, deploying its troops across the face of his battlegroup. Meyer watched as the Canadian infantry attacked into Authie against elements of 716th Infantry Division and the tanks came out of the southern side and made for Franqueville.

Throughout the night and into the morning, Battlegroup *Meyer* had been growing in strength as more troops and tanks arrived into the area. Meyer decided to put the 1st Battalion, of his 25th SS Panzergrenadier Regiment (I/25th), on his right alongside the boundary with 21st Panzer Division. II/25th Panzergrenadier Regiment was placed in front of the abbey about Cussy and St-Contest and III/25th Panzergrenadiers on his left, alongside the Caen–Bayeux highway on the north-eastern edge of Carpiquet airfield. The positions on the right and left were each backed up with two companies of Panzer IV tanks from the *Hitlerjugend* Division's 12th SS Panzer Regiment. The SS

A wounded panzergrenadier sits beside the gateway at the north entrance to Ardennes abbey. (*Bundesarchiv 146/1984/011/15A*)

HISTORY

artillery was deployed in camouflaged positions to the south-west of Caen. The start time for Battlegroup *Meyer*'s attack northwards in concert with 21st Panzer Division was set for 1600 hours, but news was coming in to Meyer's headquarters from Feuchtinger's division that its tanks and infantry were already heavily engaged in dealing with an attack by 3rd British Infantry Division on Lébisey. Meyer continued to watch the Canadians through his binoculars as they deployed their tanks and infantry in the villages in front of him, seemingly oblivious to his presence. They made a very tempting target.

Further away to the west, 7th Canadian Infantry Brigade's advance was going splendidly. By 1200 hours both the Winnipeg and Regina Rifles had reached objective Oak and were digging in around the villages of Putot-en-Bessin and Bretteville-l'Orgueilleuse, with the Regina Rifles sending a company further on to establish itself in Norrey-en-Bessin, 1 km to the south. The brigade was now just 3 km to the west of Carpiquet airfield. The division's other brigade, 8th Canadian Infantry Brigade, was still dealing with isolated pockets of resistance by-passed the day before. The Queen's Own Rifles and Régiment de la Chaudière

A captured German 50-mm anti-tank gun, which formed part of the outer defences of the radar station at Douvres. *(IWM B6315)*

tackled snipers and mopped up the areas around Colomby-sur-Thaon and Anguerny, spending the day as the divisional reserve for the advance. The brigade's third battalion, the North Shore Regiment, began 7 June in Tailleville where it had spent the night. It was now given the objective of reducing the radar station 2 km to the south near Douvres.

Part of the trench system inside the radar station at Douvres after its capture. All of the bunkers and buildings on the site were connected by trenches and tunnels, leaving little visible on the surface other than radar antennae. *(IWM B6313)*

The North Shore Regiment set out on its advance to the strongpoint at 0700 hours, with its first task being the capture of the wood to the west of the radar station. Within a very short time the battalion became embroiled in close fighting with a party of Germans who appeared to hold the wood in some strength. Prepared positions and a complex network of trenches made the capture of the area very difficult and it took most of the day to clear the wood. When the battalion finally got into position to probe the radar station defences, Lt-Col D.B. Buell found that his men had been given a task beyond their capabilities.

The *Luftwaffe* radar station at Douvres was a veritable fortress of underground bunkers, guns, wire and minefields, virtually nothing of which was visible on the surface. The first three tanks that tested the outer defences were immobilised by mines; anti-tank guns damaged two others. Fire from 19th Field Regiment, RCA, and the Cameron Highlanders' heavy mortars failed to make any impression on the defenders inside their concrete bunkers. Brigadier Foster therefore decided to contain the enemy inside the compound until a much more powerful attack could be organised. Here the Germans stayed for another ten days until a full-blown assault was mounted. Throughout this period the garrison carefully monitored all Allied movements in the area and relayed them to the German forces defending Caen. On 17 June, specialised armour from 80th Assault Squadron, RE, backed up by 41 RM Commando and supported by a heavy artillery barrage, attacked the radar station in a well-planned operation. The strongpoint was taken with the loss of only three men.

A massively reinforced barrack room shelter at the radar station at Douvres. Significant damage has been done to the roof of the building, either by bombs during an air raid or by a large charge placed by Royal Engineers during the attack on the site on 17 June. *(Author)*

Back on the coast, 48 RM Commando was still engaged in trying to reduce its D-Day objective, strongpoint WN-26 at Langrune. Lt-Col Moulton's men had spent the night looking in two directions. To their front, they contained the Germans holed up in the coastal stronghold and to their right-rear, they prepared themselves to receive a tank attack. 21st Panzer Division's drive that had reached the sea between Lion and Luc-sur-Mer had passed within 2 km of 48 RM Commando's outposts. Moulton had been alerted by brigade to the presence of these tanks on his flank and had been told to expect an attack, but the night passed quietly, for the panzers and their accompanying panzergrenadiers had withdrawn to positions north of Caen.

On the morning of 7 June Moulton's commandos tried once again to capture the Langrune strongpoint. This time they had the help of two Wolverine tank destroyers from 3rd Canadian Infantry Division's anti-tank battalion. The self-propelled guns fired solid shot into the concrete barricade barring entry into the fortification and gradually broke it down to a point where an assault could be made. A Sherman tank firing high explosive led the commandos into the maze of tunnels and bunkers and the garrison quickly surrendered to the determined marines. 48 RM Commando had finally taken one of its D-Day objectives. However, the other main objective, the joining up of Juno and Sword Beaches, was not completed until much later by another commando. 46 RM Commando had landed on 7 June and came through Langrune to take over the task of joining the beaches together. Before it could do this, however, it had to reduce the strongpoint in the next village along the coast at Luc-sur-Mer.

German prisoners being marched back through the streets of St-Aubin after 48 RM Commando captured the strongpoint at Langrune. *(IWM B5229)*

By 1400 hours, 9th Canadian Infantry Brigade's move southwards had almost reached the Caen–Bayeux road and its lead units were overlooking the hangars on Carpiquet airfield.

HISTORY

A Squadron, Sherbrooke Fusiliers, and some light Stuart tanks of its reconnaissance troop, were now concentrated around Franqueville. Behind them, C Company, North Nova Scotia Highlanders, held Authie. The rest of the battalion was further behind in Buron and in the area between the two villages, supported on each flank by more Sherbrooke Fusiliers tanks.

Kurt Meyer was still watching the advance from the abbey tower at Ardennes. The Canadians' extended left flank was strung out before him along a 3-km line of advance directly across his front. The moment had come to act. With the agreement of his divisional commander, Meyer launched his battlegroup against 9th Canadian Infantry Brigade. First into action was III/25th SS Panzergrenadier Regiment backed up by the divisional artillery and II/12th SS Panzer Regiment. They hit the exposed Sherbrooke Fusiliers in Franqueville and swept them aside, continuing the German drive into and around Authie. Here they virtually annihilated C Company, North Nova Scotia Highlanders, and pressed on out of the village towards Buron. More of the teenage *Waffen-SS* troops attacked Authie and Buron from Cussy, hitting the left flank of the Canadians with great force. In the wheat fields between the two villages vicious hand-to-hand fighting broke out as the Germans forced their way into the North Nova Scotia Highlanders' positions. The Sherbrooke Fusiliers tried to give support by sending C Squadron down the left flank, but the Shermans were quickly embroiled in a battle for their own survival when they were attacked by Panzer IVs and anti-tank guns. One after another the Canadian tanks were hit and burst into flames. For the next two hours a tank versus tank battle raged in the fields between Authie and Buron, whilst the panzergrenadiers fought their way across the open ground and into Buron itself.

When Battlegroup *Meyer* hit the exposed units of 9th Canadian Infantry Brigade the Canadians found themselves without artillery support. Unbelievably, the brigade had advanced that morning with its assigned field regiment of artillery in the previous day's positions far to the rear. At 0745 hours, when the move began, 14th Field Regiment, RCA, was located in an area to the north of Bény. By the time the North Nova Scotia Highlanders had reached Buron, the battalion had passed out of range of these guns. It was not until 1200 hours that 14th Field Regiment began to move to a new gun area 2 km to the south near Basly. Even here the guns were still over 9,500 metres from Authie, with the maximum effective range of the Priests being only 9,000 metres. To make matters worse, communications with the warships at sea were out. One of the great advantages that the Allies brought to Normandy was the overwhelming fire support of their artillery and warships. Here, however, in their first clash with the enemy in the field, the Canadians had to deal with a counter-attack without this support.

Canadian troops examining a damaged Panther tank near Authie. The tank is from 4th Company, 12th SS Panzer Regiment. (NAC PA-130147)

As the afternoon wore on the North Nova Scotia Highlanders were driven out of Buron and withdrew into an area south of les Buissons, almost back to the start line from which they advanced early that morning. By this time effective Allied artillery fire had at last come into play and was boosted with heavy calibre fire from warships. The Germans' positions were subjected to concentrated shelling, which caused their advance to falter. Meyer had further concerns when he realised also that Canadian tanks and infantry had arrived in Bretteville-l'Orgueilleuse and were now threatening his left flank. His right flank was also in action, since I/25th Panzergrenadier Regiment had attacked 9th Infantry Brigade (of 3rd British Division) when its advance units

HISTORY

The courtyard of Ardennes abbey. It was through the archway in the corner that Canadian prisoners were led into a tiny garden to the rear and executed. *(Author)*

tried to capture Cambes-en-Plaine, to the north-east of Buron. The whole of Battlegroup *Meyer* was now in combat and was meeting determined resistance. Feuchtinger's 21st Panzer Division was of little help to Meyer as it was trying to counter 3rd British Infantry Division's advance at Lébisey. Witt decided that Meyer's advance was in danger of being overwhelmed. He ordered Meyer to break off his attack and switch to defence.

In the late afternoon the North Nova Scotia Highlanders counter-attacked Buron and recaptured the village. At dusk, however, Brigadier Cunningham ordered that this advance outpost be given up and the remnants of the battalion were withdrawn into les Buissons. Here 9th Canadian Infantry Brigade dug itself into a well defended position and anchored the east face of the Canadian lodgement for the night.

The battle had been very costly for the Canadians. The North Shore Regiment had suffered 242 casualties, 84 of whom were killed and 128 taken prisoner. The Sherbrooke Fusiliers had lost 21 tanks knocked out and 7 damaged. Out of the 60 casualties amongst the tank crews, 26 were dead. 12th SS Panzer Division also had heavy losses (86 killed, 216 wounded and 27 missing) in this, its first action. Anger at these losses may partly account for the behaviour of some of its troops in the hours that followed the battle. Many of the captured Canadians were slain in cold blood after their surrender in Authie and Buron. Twenty-three specific murders were identified as having taken place in those two villages and a further 18 men were executed in the garden of Meyer's headquarters at Ardennes abbey. For these and other crimes Meyer was tried by the Canadians in December 1945. He was found guilty and sentenced to death, but this was later commuted to life imprisonment. He was released in 1954.

CHAPTER 6

COUNTER-ATTACKS AND STALEMATE

3rd Canadian Infantry Division spent the night of 7–8 June with 7th Canadian Infantry Brigade holding the west of its lodgement, with the Winnipeg Rifles in Putot and Regina Rifles in Norrey and Bretteville-l'Orgueilleuse. It had loosely linked up with troops from 50th (Northumbrian) Division to the west of Putot and north of Brouay. On the division's east flank, 9th Canadian Infantry Brigade held the area of Anisy and Villons-les-Buissons with its front line at les Buissons. Between the two brigades was an area of open country along the Mue valley, held by no one but covered by artillery located in Bray and a Canadian Scottish company in Cairon. 8th Canadian Infantry Brigade was still in reserve close to the beaches.

At 1100 hours on 8 June, Maj-Gen Keller held a conference of his brigadiers and outlined his plans for that day. 51st (Highland) Division was landing over Mike Beach and would take over responsibility for the rear area from Douvres to Courseulles, including the troublesome radar station. 9th Canadian Infantry Brigade would attack and retake Buron that day supported by the whole of the division's artillery; this attack was later postponed and eventually cancelled. The other two brigades would hold their present positions. 8th Canadian Infantry Brigade could be brought into the centre of the division's line if required. But even as he spoke, 7th Canadian Infantry Brigade was fighting furiously to resist an attack against its positions by SS panzergrenadiers.

During 7 June the remainder of 12th SS Panzer Division had continued to arrive in the area to the south-west of Caen. By the

HISTORY

Panzer IV of 9th Company, 12th SS Panzer Regiment, taking shelter in an orchard close to the front line. *(Bundesarchiv 1011/738/0271/08)*

end of the day it was almost complete and deployed in the line. Meyer's 25th SS Panzergrenadier Regiment was established in front of 9th Canadian Brigade and 9th British Brigade to the east of Caen. *SS-Standartenführer* (Colonel) Wilhelm Mohnke had brought his 26th SS Panzergrenadier Regiment forward to a position on the division's left flank in front of 7th Canadian Infantry Brigade in the villages of St-Manvieu-Norrey, le Mesnil-Patry and Cristot, opposite the Winnipeg Rifles and Regina Rifles. Most of 12th SS Panzer Regiment, commanded by *SS-Obersturmbannführer* (Lt-Col) Max Wünsche, had also completed its arrival and was dispersed in the centre of the division. Panzer Lehr Division was beginning to assemble further to the west opposite 50th (Northumbrian) Division, around Tilly-sur-Seulles.

In the early hours of 8 June, 26th SS Panzergrenadier Regiment attacked 7th Canadian Infantry Brigade. From positions north of Cheux at 0300 hours, I/26th moved against the Regina Rifles in Norrey-en-Bessin. One of I/26th SS Panzergrenadier Regiment's companies managed to get into the hamlet of Cardonville between Norrey and Bretteville-l'Orgueilleuse, but the main attack failed to seize Norrey or to reach the Caen–Bayeux railway line. To the west, II/26th SS Panzergrenadier Regiment's attack against the Winnipeg Rifles in Putot-en-Bessin was more successful. The Winnipeg battalion held Putot with three companies dug in along the railway line to the south of the village and D Company and battalion headquarters established to the east of the village. The panzergrenadiers advanced just after dawn, at around 0630 hours, but the attack was beaten off. They tried again and again throughout the morning and gradually began penetrating into the Winnipeg Rifles' lines and around the important bridge over the railway cutting to the west of the village. The close fighting continued into the afternoon, with the

Senior officers of 12th SS Panzer Division *Hitlerjugend* discuss the situation around Ardennes abbey during 9 June. Left to right: Max Wünsche, Fritz Witt, and Kurt Meyer. Wünsche had been wounded during the attack on Bretteville-l'Orgueilleuse the night before. *(Bundesarchiv 146/1988/028/25A)*

Canadians stubbornly refusing to give up their positions. The SS troops got through an underpass beneath the railway line and into Putot, slipping between the hard-pressed Winnipeg Rifles companies and encircling their isolated slit trenches. By late afternoon the Canadians were all but surrounded and almost out of ammunition. The three companies tried to withdraw under the cover of smoke, but only a few men got back to battalion headquarters just east of the village where D Company was still almost intact. Putot had been lost to II/26th SS Panzergrenadiers.

Almost immediately, Brigadier Foster ordered a counter-attack to retake the village. He brought up 1st Canadian Scottish and sent the battalion forward at 2030 hours with strong support from 1st Hussars Sherman tanks. Behind a rolling barrage laid down by 12th and 13th Field Regiments, the Canadian Scottish advanced across open cornfields towards Putot-en-Bessin, into the face of withering machine-gun fire. The Germans fought tenaciously to hold on to their gains, but the determined Canadians gave them no respite. An hour later the Canadian Scottish reported that they were in the village and mopping up enemy stragglers. The great weight of fire and the presence of tanks had forced the panzergrenadiers to withdraw. A short time later the Canadians were back in the slit trenches of the Winnipeg Rifles' original positions along the railway line, but the cost had been high. The Canadian Scottish had suffered 125 casualties in taking Putot, of whom 45 were dead. It had been even worse for the Winnipeg Rifles earlier in the day. Their losses in the battle to hold the village amounted to 256, of whom 105 were killed. This figure included a large number of men murdered after their capture, when 45 Canadians were butchered by the Hitler Youth, many of them in the grounds of the château at Audrieu.

26th SS Panzergrenadier Regiment's attack against 7th Canadian Infantry Brigade was a local push designed to eliminate the salient that the Canadians had made across the Caen–Bayeux road. Panzer Lehr Division was to attack at the same time to the west with a more ambitious objective of reaching the coast, but it had still not completed its move into the area during 8 June. In consequence it, too, made local attacks only, with incomplete units and with negligible results, against 50th Division in the vicinity of Audrieu and Brouay. The Germans were making the mistake of attacking the Allied lodgement with under-strength forces as they arrived, rather than waiting until I SS Panzer Corps was completely assembled and ready for a decisive armour strike.

12th SS Panzer Division's impatience to get at the Canadians was again demonstrated later on 8 June at Bretteville-l'Orgueilleuse. At the same time in the evening that 1st Canadian Scottish attacked Putot, 25th SS Panzergrenadier Regiment's Motorcycle Reconnaissance Company and two Panther companies of Wünsche's 12th SS Panzer Regiment were preparing to launch an attack along the Caen–Bayeux highway against the Regina Rifles in Bretteville. Meyer had decided that 9th Canadian Infantry Brigade was unlikely to attack his positions in Buron. He resolved to thrust towards Bayeux to meet up with Mohnke's 26th SS Panzergrenadier Regiment, taking the villages of Rots, Villeneuve and Bretteville on the way, while Mohnke's men attacked Norrey. This would capture an area along the Caen–Bayeux road from which 12th SS Panzer Division and Panzer Lehr Division could launch major attacks up the Seulles and Mue valleys towards Courseulles.

Men of the Regina Rifles guarding a position in Cardonville, to the south of Bretteville-l'Orgueilleuse during 12th SS Panzer Division's attacks of 8–9 June. (Donald J. Grant, NAC PA-129042)

The attack began just as daylight was fading, a company of Panther tanks carrying the motorcycle riflemen from Franqueville along either side of the Caen–Bayeux road. They crossed the River Mue at le Bourg and swept on down the road towards Bretteville. The Regina Rifles had placed a screen of anti-tank guns from 3rd Anti-Tank Regiment, RCA, on the eastern side of the village and reinforced this position with an infantry company. As soon as the Panthers came into range they were met by a barrage of anti-tank and machine-gun fire. The first two tanks to reach the edge of the village were hit and burst into flames. The SS riflemen dismounted from the tanks and advanced on foot.

There followed a confused and bitter battle as the Panthers circled round the outskirts of Bretteville, firing wildly into the darkness against real and imaginary Canadian positions. Anti-tank fire caught them in the flanks and sent tank after tank bursting into flames but German infantry penetrated into the village and fought a running battle with the Regina Rifles. Two Panthers then came straight down the main road towards the church. The leading Panther almost reached the Regina Rifles' battalion HQ before it was knocked out by an intrepid rifleman with a hand-held PIAT (Projector Infantry Anti-Tank). The following tank tried to fire its gun at the Canadian infantry but only succeeded in blowing a hole in the turret of the blazing Panther. It then retreated quickly back up the main road to safety. The battle continued through the night for over six hours amidst the burning buildings of Bretteville before the signal to recall the German force to Rots was given. I/26th SS Panzergrenadier Regiment's attack on Norrey had also failed without gaining any ground, though the Germans had successfully occupied and held the Villeneuve and Rots area in the Mue valley. German losses during these attacks totalled 152, of whom 43 were dead.

Destroyed Panther tank from 1st Battalion, 12th SS Panzer Regiment, knocked out by a PIAT opposite the Regina Rifles HQ in Bretteville-l'Orgueilleuse on 8 June. (Frank L. Dubervill, NAC PA-130149)

The Germans tried again on 9 June with the newly arrived Panthers of 3rd Company, I/12th Panzer Regiment. The company had moved into the area too late to join in the attack on Bretteville, so it was to be thrown into a new attack against

Norrey, planned for around noon. Meyer had decided that the Regina Rifles would not anticipate another attack so soon after the failure of the night before, so 3rd Company, I/12th, would move against Norrey-en-Bessin along the southern edge of the Caen–Bayeux railway, shielded from Bretteville by the line. Simultaneously, I/26th SS Panzergrenadier Regiment would again try to gain entry to Norrey from the south.

The Panthers assembled in Villeneuve, drove beneath the railway through an underpass south of the village and deployed in line abreast. At 1230 hours the 12 tanks began their attack, driving at full speed towards the gap between Norrey and Bretteville. About 1,000 metres short of the road that linked the villages, the tanks began a wide turn to the left to bear down on Norrey; it was then that the Canadians opened fire. Tank and anti-tank guns tore into the Panthers, knocking seven of them out. The other five turned around and retreated in disorder, leaving 16 Germans dead and missing, with a further 17 wounded. I/26th SS Panzergrenadier Regiment's attack against Norrey from the south also failed.

It had been an extraordinary three days for 3rd Canadian Infantry Division. Its brigades had endured fierce counter-attacks by one of Germany's crack divisions and had survived, with little danger of the enemy breaking through to the beaches. Counter-attacks were to be expected, but these strikes gave the impression of being hasty and ineffectively improvised. As the Canadian official history explained: 'The attacks were pressed with courage and determination but with no particular tactical skill.' The Germans had flung themselves straight against the strongest points and had failed to exploit the weakness of their opponents' positions. 12th SS Panzer Division's setbacks reinforced the maxim that strength should not be risked by launching it in 'penny packets', but kept intact for striking a decisive and massive blow. 12th SS Panzer Division now went over on to the defensive, awaiting the moment that a combined panzer force of several divisions could be launched against the landings.

On the Canadian side, the attack to retake Buron was postponed indefinitely. The left of the division's front line would remain anchored on les Buissons. Any further advance south would lengthen and expose this flank until 3rd British Infantry Division could move forward from Cambes and come into line in front of Caen to protect it. On 10 June it was decided that the

Scene in Bretteville-l'Orgueilleuse after the battle of 8–9 June. *(NAC PA-133732)*

position in Norrey be extended to the high ground beyond Cheux, 4 km to the south. Before this could be done, however, the Germans had to be cleared from the Mue valley and removed from Rots to close the gap between 7th and 9th Canadian Infantry Brigades. This attack was planned for 11 June and the move south from Norrey was to be carried out a day later.

46 RM Commando was given the main task of clearing the Mue valley. Landing on 7 June, the commando had been involved in clearing the Luc-sur-Mer strongpoint and linking the Juno and Sword landings. Since then it had been holding part of the perimeter round the Douvres radar station. The commando now came under 8th Canadian Infantry Brigade's command for the attack. 46 RM Commando was to move into the valley from Thaon and clear the few German stragglers from the villages of Cairon, Lasson and Rosel, before attacking the panzergrenadiers holed up in Rots. The commando would have the support of the Fort Garry Horse's tanks for the advance. The North Shore Regiment and Régiment de la Chaudière would then move into the valley behind them and hold the ground.

The attack began on 11 June and proceeded as planned. 46 RM Commando took the first three villages in the Mue valley against little opposition. Then the commando met the fanatical *Waffen-SS* men in and around Rots during the late afternoon.

The Royal Marines advanced on either side of the diminutive River Mue and clashed with the panzergrenadiers as they approached the houses of Rots. Fighting in and amongst the village buildings was vicious and costly and continued for the rest of the day and into the night. The Fort Garry Horse Shermans advanced into Rots along the main road from the north and were met by Panther tanks in the centre. A short struggle in the square by the church resulted in three of the Canadian tanks being knocked out. The defenders then destroyed a further three Shermans before the Canadians took the village. The commandos suffered alarming casualties as they pressed on through Rots and along the west side of the valley, clearing the tiny village of le Hamel as they went. Fighting from house to house, they were in continuous close contact with the enemy. The dead were left lying body to body. It was the early hours of the 12th before the area was deemed to be clear of the Germans, although they were still close by in some strength at Villeneuve. When the men of the Régiment de la Chaudière consolidated in the ruins of Rots, they counted 122 German bodies buried in the rubble, although German records show that 12th SS Panzer Division had suffered 22 dead, 30 wounded and 15 missing during the battle. 46 RM Commando's losses were 22 dead and over 80 wounded.

8th Canadian Infantry Brigade's move from Norrey-en-Bessin towards Cheux, planned for 12 June, was hurriedly brought forward to 11 June in order to coincide with a 50th Division attack on the right. The plan was for the 1st Hussars and Queen's Own Rifles to attack from Norrey-en-Bessin through le Mesnil-Patry and then southwards, to seize the high ground beyond Cheux. The village itself was to be by-passed. The remainder of 2nd Canadian Armoured Brigade was then to come forward and establish itself on the final objective.

The Canadian advance began at 1430 hours on 11 June. B Squadron, 1st Hussars, led the attack with the men of D Company, Queen's Own Rifles, riding on the backs of its Shermans. Once clear of Norrey the tanks moved out across the cornfields towards le Mesnil-Patry, 2 km away. Half-way across the open ground the Canadian force met heavy mortar and machine-gun fire, forcing the infantry to dismount and go to ground. The B Squadron tanks then split in two with two troops swinging to the right towards an orchard to the north of the village. The remainder pushed on through slit trenches on the

HISTORY

outskirts of le Mesnil-Patry in an effort to get to grips with the Germans. Anti-tank fire ripped into the Shermans. Those that gained le Mesnil-Patry came into contact with a large body of German tanks and more anti-tank guns. Within minutes numbers of Shermans were burning furiously. On the northern side of the village the other group of the 1st Hussars met more opposition when three Panzer IVs hit the Canadians in the flank, knocking out six Shermans.

C Squadron was then ordered forward into the mêlée. Its tanks swept at speed across the open ground from Norrey and accounted for large numbers of enemy infantry before a second company of Panzer IVs struck their left flank. Amid more anti-tank shells, more hits and more burning Shermans, 1st Hussars' commanding officer, Lt-Col L.R.J. Colwell, realised that the situation was becoming critical. He had lost the best part of two squadrons and was in grave danger of being completely outflanked. He therefore ordered his force to disengage and withdraw to the start line. B Squadron did not receive the message, however, and virtually the whole of its complement of Shermans was destroyed in the village. All of B Squadron's officers and all save three of its NCOs were listed as missing. Only three tanks returned to Norrey. C Squadron suffered equally alarming losses with only seven of its tanks returning safely. The supporting infantry fared little better, for they were caught in the open by heavy mortar and machine-gun fire and were decimated. D Company, Queen's Own Rifles of Canada, suffered 96 casualties, more than half of whom were killed or missing. In all 114 of the total of 179 casualties taken in the attack were dead. The attack on le Mesnil-Patry had been a complete and costly failure.

2nd Canadian Armoured Brigade's failed attack on le Mesnil-Patry on 11 June was the last major operation attempted by 3rd Canadian Infantry Division that month. The day also marked the end of the first stage of the invasion. By the night of 11 June the Allies had 326,547 men, 54,186 vehicles and 104,428 tons of stores ashore in Normandy. The strength of the Allied forces in France meant that the lodgement was now firmly established and unlikely to be eliminated.

Two artificial harbours were being built, one at Arromanches and another off Omaha Beach. Once completed, they would allow the landing of further reinforcements and stores to increase

Then: The town square by the church at Rots after its capture by 46 Royal Marine Commando. One of the three Fort Garry Horse Shermans that were knocked out here by a single Panther can be seen on the right. *(Frank L. Dubervill, NAC PA-115533)*

Now: The Rots town square today. *(Author)*

in pace. On 11 June Airfield B3 at Ste-Croix opened and, for the first time since 1940, the RAF was operating from French soil.

It had been an eventful six days for 3rd Canadian Infantry Division, starting with its successful breaking of the Atlantic Wall defences on Juno Beach on 6 June and ending with a humiliating defeat in an inland village on 11 June. During this period the division and its attached troops had suffered 2,832 casualties, 1,117 of whom were killed.

Memorial to 46 RM Commando in the hamlet of le Hamel on the western side of the River Mue opposite Rots. *(Author)*

Over the next week or so there was some minor realignment of the line. Le Mesnil-Patry was occupied without casualties on 17 June when the Germans withdrew from the village before being outflanked by a British advance to the west. 8th Canadian Infantry Brigade relieved 7th Canadian Infantry Brigade in Putot, Bretteville and Norrey and Brigadier Foster's tired battalions went into reserve.

The battle for Normandy continued into August before the German line began to crack; week after week of bloody battles and devastating destruction. Throughout the Allies continued to build up their strength over the beaches and through the single artificial harbour that had survived gale-force winds. The number of Allied troops ashore expanded at a rate that outmatched the Germans' ability to reinforce their formations. The brutal attrition in the close confines of the Normandy countryside ground down the Germans to a point where they broke and retreated in disorder, leaving their Seventh Army destroyed on the battlefield.

PART THREE

BATTLEFIELD TOURS

GENERAL TOURING INFORMATION

Normandy is a thriving holiday area, with some beautiful countryside, excellent beaches and very attractive architecture (particularly in the case of religious buildings). It was also, of course, the scene of heavy fighting in 1944, and this has had a considerable impact on the tourist industry. To make the most of your trip, especially if you intend visiting non-battlefield sites, we strongly recommend you purchase one of the general Normandy guidebooks that are commonly available. These include: *Michelin Green Guide: Normandy*; *Thomas Cook Travellers: Normandy*; *The Rough Guide to Brittany and Normandy*; *Lonely Planet: Normandy*.

TRAVEL REQUIREMENTS

First, make sure you have the proper documentation to enter France as a tourist. Citizens of European Union countries, including Great Britain, should not usually require visas, but will need to carry and show their passports. Others should check with the French Embassy in their own country before travelling. British citizens should also fill in and take Form E111 (available from main post offices), which deals with entitlement to medical treatment, and all should consider taking out comprehensive travel insurance. France is part of the Eurozone, and you should also check exchange rates before travelling.

GETTING THERE

The most direct routes from the UK to Lower Normandy are by ferry from Portsmouth to Ouistreham (near Caen), and from Portsmouth or Poole to Cherbourg. Depending on which you choose, and whether you travel by day or night, the crossing takes between five and seven hours. Alternatively, you can sail to Le Havre, Boulogne or Calais and drive the rest of the way. (Travel time from Calais to Caen is about four hours; motorway and bridge tolls may be payable depending on the exact route taken.) Another option is to use the Channel Tunnel. Whichever way you choose to travel, early booking is advised, especially during the summer months.

Although you can of course hire motor vehicles in Normandy, the majority of visitors from the UK or other EU countries will probably take their own. If you do so, you will also need to take: a full driving licence; your vehicle registration document; a certificate of motor insurance valid in France (your insurer will advise on this); spare headlight and indicator bulbs; headlight beam adjusters or tape; a warning triangle; and a sticker or number plate identifying which country the vehicle is registered in. Visitors from elsewhere should consult a motoring organisation in their home country for details of the documents and other items they will require.

Above: Monument to the landings and the liberation of Europe at the main exit from Mike Red Beach to the west of Courseulles. *(Author)*

Page 95: A 2nd Canadian Armoured Brigade 17-pounder Sherman Firefly tank moving across open ground near Buron. *(Ken Bell, NAC PA-131391)*

The Normandy road system is well developed, although there are still a few choke points, especially around the larger towns during rush hour and in the holiday season. As a general guide, in clear conditions it is possible to drive from Cherbourg to Caen in less than two hours.

ACCOMMODATION

Accommodation in Normandy is plentiful and diverse, from cheap campsites to five star hotels in glorious châteaux. However, early booking is advised if you wish to travel between June and August. There is no shortage of places to stay in the Juno Beach area and, as you would expect from a holiday region, there are plenty of good cafés and restaurants nearby. All of the seaside towns have hotels, mostly small to medium in size and rather reminiscent of an earlier age. Nonetheless, they are welcoming, comfortable and often complete with their own excellent restaurants. Most towns in the area have websites where you can find a list of available hotels and compare prices and facilities before you book. For those who wish to stay in modern large hotels that are usually part of a chain or group, there are quite a number located just a few kilometres inland around Caen, just inside the ring road. There are four or five within about a kilometre of the *Mémorial de Caen* alone. These offer a full range of facilities and are clean and comfortable, if a little impersonal. The excellent roads nearby make access from Caen to Juno Beach and the sites covered in the tours extremely easy.

The old *Hôtel de la Plage* just off the beach at Bernières which briefly became Maj-Gen Keller's forward command post on D-Day. *(Author)*

If you decide to pay a sudden visit to the area without booking in advance, then all of the local tourist offices (*Les Syndicats d'Initiatives*) have leaflets listing nearby hotels and will help you locate a suitable place to stay. But please do not chance this during the days close to 6 June, or in July and August, for most of the hotels will be fully booked. An alternative is to consider renting a *gîte* or apartment and making your stay a little longer, combining a beach holiday with a pilgrimage to the battlefields. Brittany Ferries supply a brochure listing some of those available in the area, as do other ferry and travel companies.

Useful contacts include:

French Travel Centre, 178 Piccadilly, London W1V 0AL;
  tel: 0870 830 2000; web: www.raileurope.co.uk
Calvados Tourisme, Place du Canada, 14000 Caen;
  tel: +33 (0)2 31 86 53 30; web: www.calvados-tourisme.com

Manche Tourisme; web: www.manchetourisme.com
Maison du Tourisme de Cherbourg et du Haut-Cotentin,
2 Quai Alexandre III, 50100 Cherbourg-Octeville;
tel: +33 (0)2 33 93 52 02; web: www.ot-cherbourg-cotentin.fr
Gîtes de France, La Maison des Gîtes de France et du Tourisme
Vert, 59 rue Saint-Lazare, 75 439 Paris Cedex 09;
tel: +33 (0)1 49 70 75 75; web: www.gites-de-france.fr

Maj-Gen Keller and some of his staff come ashore on Nan White Beach at Bernières on the morning of D-Day. (*NAC PA-115534*)

BATTLEFIELD TOURING

Each volume in the 'Battle Zone Normandy' series contains from four to six battlefield tours. These are intended to last from a few hours to a full day apiece. Some are best undertaken using motor transport, others should be done on foot, and many involve a mixture of the two. Owing to its excellent infrastructure and relatively gentle topography, Normandy also makes a good location for a cycling holiday; indeed, some of the tours are ideally suited to this method.

In every case the tour author has visited the area concerned recently, so the information presented should be accurate and reasonably up to date. Nevertheless land use, infrastructure and rights of way can change, sometimes at short notice. If you encounter difficulties in following any tour, we would very much like to hear about it, so we can incorporate changes in future

BATTLEFIELD TOURS

editions. Your comments should be sent to the publisher at the address provided at the front of this book.

To derive maximum value and enjoyment from the tours, we suggest you equip yourself with the following items:

- Appropriate maps. European road atlases can be purchased from a wide range of locations outside France. However, for navigation within Normandy, the French Institut Géographique National (IGN: <www.ign.fr>) produces maps at a variety of scales. The 1:100,000 series ('Top 100') is particularly useful when driving over larger distances; sheet 06 (Caen – Cherbourg) covers most of the invasion area. For pinpointing locations precisely, the current IGN 1:25,000 Série Bleue is best (we use extracts from this series for the tour maps in this book). These can be purchased in many places across Normandy. They can also be ordered in the UK from some high street bookshops, or from specialist map dealers such as the Hereford Map Centre, 24–25 Church Street, Hereford HR1 2LR; tel: 01432 266322; web: <www.themapcentre.com>. Allow at least a fortnight's notice, although some maps may be in stock.
- Lightweight waterproof clothing and robust footwear are essential, especially for touring in the countryside.
- Take a compass, provided you know how to use one!
- A camera and spare films/memory cards.
- A notebook and writing materials to record what you have photographed.
- A French dictionary and/or phrasebook. (English is widely spoken in the coastal area, but is much less common inland.)
- Food and drink. Although you are never very far in Normandy from a shop, restaurant or *tabac*, many of the tours do not pass directly by such facilities. It is therefore sensible to take some light refreshment with you.
- Binoculars. Most officers and some other ranks carried binoculars in 1944. Taking a pair adds a surprising amount of verisimilitude to the touring experience.

SOME DO'S AND DON'TS

Battlefield touring can be an extremely interesting and even emotional experience, especially if you have read something about the battles beforehand. In addition, it is fair to say that

Nan White Beach at Bernières seen from the position of the strongpoint in the centre of the Queen's Own Rifles' landings. The concrete structure on the left is a mortar position. The house on the left in the middle distance is by the main exit from the beach and features prominently in many contemporary photographs of the invasion. *(Author)*

residents of Normandy are used to visitors, among them battlefield tourists, and generally will do their best to help if you encounter problems. However, many of the tours in the 'Battle Zone Normandy' series are off the beaten track, and you can expect some puzzled looks from the locals, especially inland. In all cases we have tried to ensure that tours are on public land, or viewable from public rights of way. In the unlikely event that you are asked to leave a site, do so immediately and by the most direct route.

In addition: **Never remove 'souvenirs' from the battlefields.** Even today it is not unknown for farmers to turn up relics of the 1944 fighting. Taking these without permission may not only be illegal, but can be extremely dangerous. It also ruins the site for genuine battlefield archaeologists. Anyone returning from France should also remember customs regulations on the import of weapons and ammunition of any kind.

Be especially careful when investigating fortifications. Some of the more frequently-visited sites are well preserved, and several of them have excellent museums. However, both along the coast and inland, there are numerous positions that have been left to decay, and which carry risks for the unwary. In particular, remember

The harbour entrance and estuary of the River Seulles at Courseulles. The picture was taken on the afternoon of D-Day with the tide half out. The earlier high tide has allowed two large tank landing ships to beach near the high water mark at the top of Mike Red Beach. *(IWM CL40)*

that many of these places were the scenes of heavy fighting or subsequent demolitions, which may have caused severe (and sometimes invisible) structural damage. Coastal erosion has also undermined the foundations of a number of shoreline defences. Under no circumstances should underground bunkers, chambers and tunnels be entered, and care should always be taken when examining above-ground structures. If in any doubt, stay away.

Beware of hunting (shooting) areas (sign-posted *Chasse Gardée*). Do not enter these, even if they offer a short cut to your destination. Similarly, Normandy contains a number of restricted areas (military facilities and wildlife reserves), which should be avoided. Watch out, too, for temporary footpath closures, especially along sections of coastal cliffs.

If using a motor vehicle, keep your eyes on the road. There are many places to park, even on minor routes, and it is always better to turn round and retrace your path than to cause an accident. In rural areas avoid blocking entrances and driving along farm tracks; again, it is better to walk a few hundred metres than to cause damage and offence.

The stretch of coastline around Juno Beach is very popular in summer, but still relatively uncrowded. Out of season the coast and the surrounding area are perfect places to walk, explore and take in the agreeable pursuits of exercise, fresh air and good food. The beaches here are wide, flat and sandy, excellent for families. None of these bathing places are over-commercialised, and the resorts rely mainly on the natural attractions of sun, sea and sand, rather than more developed pastimes. In the evenings, the casinos at Riva Bella, Luc-sur-Mer and St-Aubin-sur-Mer offer a more adult type of entertainment. All along the coast here it is still possible to drive your car right up to the edge of the sands, park without payment and enjoy a day on the beach.

For those who wish to experience more of Normandy than the 1944 battlefields, the area is also rich in more distant relics of the past, together with many modern attractions. As always, the local tourist office should be your first port of call, to pick up leaflets describing suitable places to visit. Caen and Bayeux are excellent venues in which to spend a day; both are full of cultural sites, fascinating buildings, interesting streets and wonderful restaurants. There are thriving markets at Caen, Ouistreham/Riva Bella and Courseulles, selling a full range of fresh Norman produce and other items.

BATTLEFIELD TOURS

View of the car park close by the harbour entrance at Courseulles, the starting point for all of the tours. (Author)

All of the tours in this book are designed to be practicable by car or bicycle. They are all relatively short with the longest being around 48 km (30 miles). They all begin at the tiny port of Courseulles located in the middle of Juno Beach. The town is situated 16 km north-west of the centre of Caen and 15 km west of Ouistreham. Courseulles is a thriving fishing port and holiday centre with a wide sandy beach. To the east of the town, between Courseulles and Ouistreham, are the seaside villages and towns of Bernières, St-Aubin, Langrune, Luc-sur-Mer, Lion-sur-Mer and Riva Bella, all of which are busy holiday resorts in the summer. To the west of Courseulles the coast is less developed with the nearest town being Arromanches 10 km away, and Port-en-Bessin a further 10 km beyond that.

For the military minded, in addition to those museums and war cemeteries mentioned in the tours, the nearby attractions listed in the box opposite could also be included on your itinerary. Further afield, there are many more excellent museums relating to the American landings and to all aspects of the subsequent fighting in Normandy. Again, go to any local tourist office and pick up the booklet *The D-Day Landings and the Battle of Normandy*, which lists 35 museums and sites in the wider area that are worthy of a visit.

A WORD OF CAUTION

These tours are along roads in daily use by the local population going about their business. They will not be expecting cars in front of them to be crawling slowly along with their drivers paying more attention to the fields and hedgerows than the road ahead. If you want to examine a view or study the lay of the land, then pull over where it is safe and walk back. Take your time and consider your own safety and that of other road users.

You may find that the very best time to undertake these tours is in the early afternoon or early evening (seasons permitting) when the locals are at home preoccupied with their food. Certainly the time not to go anywhere near Caen is during the rush hour when every side road and country lane is being used as a short cut by anxious and very manic commuters.

It is also very important to respect the land and the countryside. Do not wander aimlessly across fields heavy with crops, try to keep to the footpaths and pay due regard to the laws of trespass and to privacy notices.

Military Museums of Interest

Caen Mémorial Museum of Peace, Esplanade Eisenhower, BP 6261, 14066 Caen; tel: +33 (0)2 31 06 06 44; web: <www.memorial-caen.fr>. Open: 0900–1800 daily, 15–31 Jan; 0900–1900 daily, Feb–June & Sept–Dec; 0900–2000 daily, July–Aug; closed 25 Dec & 1–15 Jan.

Mémorial Pegasus, Avenue du Major Howard, 14860 Ranville; tel: +33 (0)2 31 78 19 44; email: <memorial.pegasus@wanadoo.fr>; web: <www.normandy1944.com>. Open 0930–1830 May–Sept, 1000–1300 and 1400–1700 Oct–Nov and Feb–Apr, closed Dec and Jan.

Musée de la Batterie de Merville, Avenue de la Batterie, 14810 Merville-Franceville; tel: +33 (0)2 31 91 47 53. Open 1000–1800 Apr–Sept, 1000–1700 second half of Mar and first half Oct, closed remainder of year.

D-Day Museum Arromanches, Place du 6 Juin, 14117 Arromanches; tel: +33 (0)2 31 22 34 31; web: <www.normandy1944.com>.

Battle of Normandy Memorial Museum, Boulevard Fabian Ware, 14400 Bayeux; tel: +33 (0)2 31 51 46 90; fax: +33 (0)2 31 51 46 91.

No. 4 Commando Museum, Place Alfred Thomas, 14150 Ouistreham; tel: +33 (0)2 31 96 63 10. Open Feb to mid-Nov.

Atlantic Wall Museum, Avenue du 6 Juin, 14150 Ouistreham; tel: +33 (0)2 31 97 28 69; email: <bunkermusee@aol.com>. Open Feb to mid-Nov.

Museum of Underwater D–Day Wrecks, BP 914520, Port-en-Bessin; tel: +33 (0)2 31 21 17 06.

Longues-sur-Mer Gun Battery, 14400 Longues-sur-Mer; tel: +33 (0)2 31 06 06 44; fax: +33 (0)2 31 06 01 70; web: <www.memorial-caen.fr>.

BATTLEFIELD TOURS

BATTLEFIELD TOURS

You will find good local maps useful such as the already-mentioned 1:25,000 series published by the IGN. Two are essential for the Juno area, *1612 OT* and *1512 OT*.

TOUR A

COURSEULLES AND THE DRIVE TO CAEN

OBJECTIVE: This tour begins with the landings at Courseulles and then follows the route of 3rd Canadian Infantry Division's furthest advance on D-Day.

DURATION/SUITABILITY: The tour covers some 22 km and will probably take about half a day to complete. It is a good tour for the cyclist, moderately hilly, but with a few stretches of busy highways. It is also good for the disabled: most of the beach at Courseulles can be seen from the promenade and all other sites are accessible by car.

DIRECTIONS: Start the tour at the entrance to Courseulles harbour in the car park by the beach opposite the Maison de la Mer. Walk from the car park across to the railings that line the harbour entrance.

THE SITE: The waterway here is also the estuary of the River Seulles. The river marks the dividing line between Mike and Nan Beaches, which made up the overall landing place known as Juno Beach. Mike Beach is on the far side of the river and one of its concrete bunkers can be clearly seen. Close by the harbour entrance is a 50-mm anti-tank gun with its original shield showing signs of the Allied

The preserved 50-mm gun by the harbour at Courseulles. *(Author)*

shell-fire which knocked it out. The gun has been restored and replaced near to its original location. The picture below shows it in its wartime position sunk into a gun pit to give it a much lower silhouette.

The 50-mm anti-tank gun by the harbour entrance at Courseulles pictured shortly after the battle. *(Archives du Mémorial de Caen)*

The tank on display opposite is an original veteran of D-Day which, unfortunately, did not make it to shore for 26 years. The tank is a Duplex Drive (DD) Sherman from 6th Canadian Armoured Regiment (1st Hussars) which sank on the run-in to the beaches on D-Day and was eventually recovered from the sea in 1970. It was restored to its wartime condition and installed here as a monument to the Canadian armoured forces. The numerous plaques around the side of the tank commemorate various units involved in the campaign in Normandy.

To the left towards the Maison de la Mer is a monument commemorating the Allied liberation of France and the return of General de Gaulle on 14 June 1944.

The salvaged DD Sherman of 1st Hussars at Courseulles. *(Author)*

DIRECTIONS: Turn to the right and walk towards the

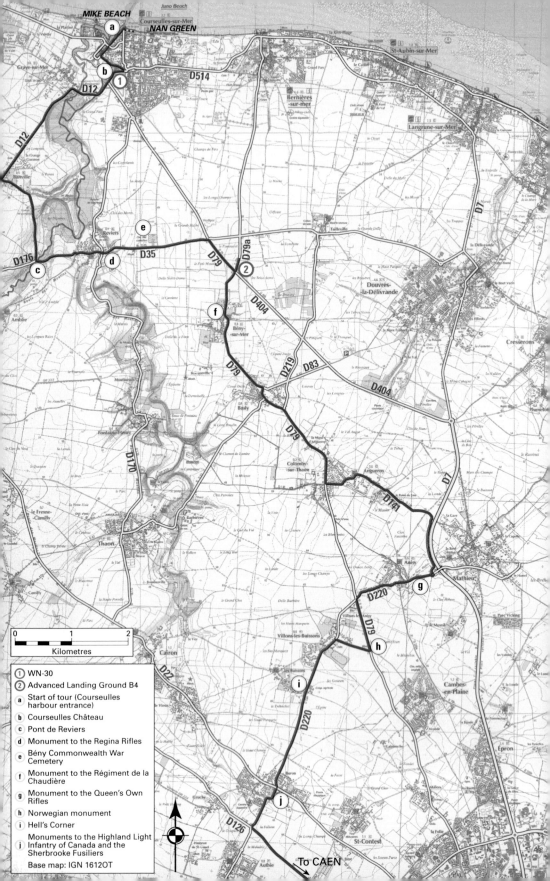

MIKE BEACH
Juno Beach
Courseulles-sur-Mer
NAN GREEN

D514

D12

D12

D176

D35

D79a

D79

D404

D219 D83

D79

D404

D170

D7

D741

D220

D79

D22

D220

D126

To CAEN

0   1   2
Kilometres

① WN-30
② Advanced Landing Ground B4
a Start of tour (Courseulles harbour entrance)
b Courseulles Château
c Pont de Reviers
d Monument to the Regina Rifles
e Bény Commonwealth War Cemetery
f Monument to the Régiment de la Chaudière
g Monument to the Queen's Own Rifles
h Norwegian monument
i Hell's Corner
j Monuments to the Highland Light Infantry of Canada and the Sherbrooke Fusiliers
Base map: IGN 1612OT

beach. Just to the right at the end of the car park is a monument to the French destroyer *Combattante*.

THE SITE: The Free French warship was part of Bombardment Force E on D-Day and, along with four Royal Navy destroyers, engaged targets on Mike and Nan Green Beaches at ranges down to 3,000 metres. On 14 June 1944 the *Combattante* brought General de Gaulle back to France from Britain and landed him near Courseulles. The ship hit a mine in February 1945 and sank with the loss of 71 of its crew, including two British seamen.

DIRECTIONS: Return to the seafront and walk to the entrance to the beach.

THE SITE: On either side of the opening through the sea wall are a number of plaques commemorating Allied units. Not all of them relate to those who landed here during the assault. There is a tablet dedicated to 1st Battalion, Canadian Scottish Regiment, which landed on the other side of the Seulles on Mike Beach, and plaques to 6th Battalion, Royal Scots, and 7th Battalion, King's Own Scottish Borderers, which landed with 15th (Scottish) Division as part of the build-up of Allied forces after D-Day. One of the plaques commemorates the assault role played by the Regina Rifles. It commemorates the 458 officers and men of the battalion who were killed during the liberation of Europe.

DIRECTIONS: Walk down the ramp and on to the beach.

THE SITE: This is the right hand sector of Nan Green Beach, the Regina Rifles' landing place. The two Regina Rifles assault companies came ashore along the main beach to the right at 0810 hours. A Company landed closest to this point, with B Company a few hundred metres further to the east. To the left, beneath the buildings which house the aquarium and the *Bar de la Mer*, is the site of a massive coast defence emplacement, which contained an 88-mm gun, sited to fire in enfilade along Nan White Beach.

> **Landing close by this point with the Regina Rifles on D-Day was Rifleman James Dunfield.**
>
> 'After the doors went down, it was every man for himself. I got about half way across the beach when the sand came

up and hit me in the face, or was it the other way around! Anyway my rifle and helmet went flying and I raised my head and my nose was bleeding. I looked around and I was just about in front of an armoured car. They let me know they knew I was there and so I felt quite safe. I was lucky it wasn't tracer that hit me as the bullet went through me from my right shoulder, breaking the clavicle, puncturing the apex of my right lung, fracturing my first and third ribs and my second vertebra and out my lower left shoulder. I'm very thankful it missed the grenades I was carrying in my haversack.'

Source: Gordon Brown and Terry Copp, *Look To Your Front . . . Regina Rifles*, p. 36.

DIRECTIONS: Return to the promenade and turn left.

THE SITE: A short distance along on the right is another monument, an impressive wooden dagger pointing skywards. This commemorates the landings made by the Royal Winnipeg Rifles, who actually made their assault on the other side of the harbour entrance over Mike Beach. You are now in the centre of strongpoint WN-29, which blocked Nan Green Beach. On either side of this monument was a complex of defence posts, linked by trenches and minefields. The inland side of the beach, between this point and the main buildings of the town, was a long anti-tank ditch with the railway line before it. Between the monument and the top of the beach along the sand dunes were several other concrete bunkers housing heavy machine guns and mortars.

DIRECTIONS: Continue along the promenade to the swimming pool and look back along the beach.

THE SITE: Between your viewpoint and the lateral road 50 metres behind you to the left was the site of a further concrete emplacement, which housed a powerful 75-mm gun. The section of beach in front of you was covered by this gun and the 88-mm gun by the harbour entrance, both housed in reinforced concrete bunkers and sited to sweep the beach with concentrated fire.

DIRECTIONS: Continue westwards along the promenade for about 50 metres and stop.

Stranded DD Sherman of 1st Hussars and a Bofors anti-aircraft gun beside a casemate at the top of Nan Green Beach. *(Frank L. Dubervill, NAC PA-132897)*

THE SITE: You are now in the centre of Nan Green Beach. B Company touched down just to the right of here during the initial assault waves. The gently sloping shoreline meant that the assault craft came to a halt in shallow water a long way out and both companies of Regina Rifles infantry had to cross more than 200 metres of open sands, criss-crossed with enemy fire and devoid of cover. Casualties on the beach were high, especially amongst A Company who landed right in front of the strongpoint to your left. The infantry got off the beach near this position and then turned right to put in a flanking attack on the strongpoint at the top of the beach, while the armour brought their fire to bear on the concrete emplacements. The infantry pressed home the assault with great bravery and determination and got amongst the wire and trenches to tackle the defenders, clearing the area with rifle and grenade. When the tanks began firing high explosive into the embrasures of the gun emplacements they quickly capitulated. After the battle both of the big gun casemates were found to have been knocked out by direct shots from DD tanks, although both had also had their concrete sides and gun shields marked by shells from naval vessels. The 75-mm gun close by where you are standing had over 200 empty shell cases lying around it, testimony to the high

Canadian troops landing over the flat sands of Nan Green Beach at Courseulles late on D-Day. The stranded tank landing craft will be floated off on the next high tide. *(Ken Bell, NAC PA-114060)*

rate of fire put up by the crew during the landings. Over on the right, B Company's troops managed to get off the beach much quicker and swung to their right to enter the built-up area of Courseulles and begin clearing the town.

DIRECTIONS: Return along the promenade to the car park. You are now going to follow a part of 7th Canadian Infantry Brigade's path inland on D-Day. Exit the car park to the right and follow the road round alongside the harbour entrance.

THE SITE: The Allies used the quays of this small port on either side of the waterway soon after the landing, but they were only suitable for unloading small craft and barges and could only land a fraction of the supplies needed to support the campaign. For the next few months, most stores and reinforcements were landed through the artificial Mulberry harbour at Arromanches and across open beaches.

DIRECTIONS: Continue straight on past the swing bridge on your right and then take the second turning on the left. Follow the road up past the château to a junction and turn right. After about 100 metres the road swings to the left and rises to a roundabout.

The estuary of the River Seulles at Courseulles looking towards the harbour entrance. The river marked the dividing line between Mike and Nan Beaches, with Mike Beach to the left and Nan Green Beach to the right. *(Author)*

THE SITE: The ground on the left opposite the cemetery was the site of strongpoint WN-30, which protected the southern edge of Courseulles. It mainly consisted of field positions of trenches and wire, strengthened with mortar and machine-gun posts. Its capture during the late morning was a relatively easy affair for the Regina Rifles assisted by some 1st Hussars tanks.

DIRECTIONS: At the roundabout, take the first exit to Banville, the D12. Follow the road until the long straight into Banville, taken by C Company, Winnipeg Rifles, which had landed with the follow-up waves on Mike Red Beach. About 100 metres before the sharp bend to the right, take the turning on the left just before the *tabac*, heading in the direction of Reviers.

THE SITE: The road now descends into the Seulles valley through some delightful countryside with the river on your left. Turn left at the road junction after about 2 km. Just in front of you is the Pont de Reviers, the bridge which crosses the River Seulles. This was an important objective for the Winnipeg Rifles as it formed an inland link between the landings that had taken place on either side of the river at Courseulles. C Company seized and held the bridge during the late morning of D-Day. 88-mm guns firing from the high ground to the right knocked out several tanks here.

DIRECTIONS: Continue along the D176 into Reviers. Pass through the village to the roundabout and take the second exit (straight on) sign-posted to the Bény Canadian Commonwealth War Cemetery. Continue up the hill out of the village along the D35 towards the war cemetery, which can be found on the left after about 1 km. There is a small lay-by in front of the entrance and a much larger car park 50 metres further on.

THE SITE: On the right a short distance from Reviers along the road to the cemetery is a memorial stone dedicated to the men of the Regina Rifles who were the first Allied troops into the village. The Regina Rifles turned to the south at the roundabout behind you and led 7th Canadian Infantry Brigade's advance up that road towards Fontaine-Henry. You are now going forward to join 8th and 9th Canadian Infantry Brigade's advance inland. 7th Canadian Infantry Brigade's route is covered in *Tour E*.

The Commonwealth War Graves Commission Cemetery at Bény-sur-Mer. *(Author)*

The Bény war cemetery is one of two Canadian cemeteries in Normandy; the other is at Cintheaux between Caen and Falaise. There are 2,048 graves here, mostly of those men killed during the landings and the first few weeks of the fighting. As with all of the Commonwealth War Cemeteries, this burial ground is laid out as an oasis of green lawns and summer flowers with a stillness that leads a visitor to deep contemplation. The setting here is perfect, situated on the top of a hill with views looking out towards the sea.

DIRECTIONS: Continue eastwards along the D35. At the road junction ahead take great care for this is the main road from Courseulles to Caen, which can be something of a race track in the late afternoon. Turn right towards Caen on the D79 and then take the next turning on the left (D79a) after about 800 metres. Pull over to the side by the monument and flagpole.

THE SITE: This memorial recollects that this open ground was the site of Advanced Landing Ground B4, completed and ready for operations nine days after the invasion. The airfield was the principal base for 126th Wing, Royal Canadian Air Force, with the Spitfires of 401, 411 and 412 Squadrons. Before the invasion, Allied planners had predicted that over 90 airfields would be needed to sustain operations in France during the first three months after the invasion. This target was reached; 90 days after the landings there were 93 Allied airfields in use in France. The landing ground here was the fourth to be completed and its single runway stretched across the area behind the monument, about 150 metres in front of where you are standing. It remained operational until 7 August 1944. The road northwards to your left leads to Bernières and it was down this route that the Régiment de la Chaudière advanced from Nan White Beach. The battalion formed up in a wood to the south of Bernières and moved through here towards Bény at around 1400 hours, accompanied by A Squadron, Fort Garry Horse. During the advance, A Company captured a two-gun battery to the north-west of where you are standing and B Company was dispatched to attack the more powerful Bény field gun battery 1.5 km to the south-west of this point.

DIRECTIONS: Turn around and go back to the road junction.

Cross over the main Courseulles–Caen road towards the village of Bény-sur-Mer. Continue along the D79 into the village and pull over opposite the church.

THE SITE: Close by is a monument to the Régiment de la Chaudière. C Company, Régiment de la Chaudière, captured Bény at about 1530 hours on 6 June. The route up from Nan Beach, where 8th Canadian Infantry Brigade landed, through Bény was also the main route forward for 3rd Canadian Infantry Division's reserve brigade, 9th Canadian Infantry Brigade. This brigade made its move inland towards its D-Day objectives on the Caen–Bayeux highway during the late afternoon. Delays in the landings and congestion on the beach meant that its lead battalion, the North Nova Scotia Highlanders, did not arrive in Bény until the early evening. By this time the Régiment de la Chaudière had moved on and liberated the next village of Basly.

DIRECTIONS: Continue on the D79 into Basly. Pull over to the right just after the church to see the monument to the liberators of the village. Continue along the D79 to Colomby-sur-Thaon.

THE SITE: On the left of the Bény–Basly road, 2 km to the north-east, is the German radar station near Douvres. Fire from this heavily defended position caused problems for the advancing Canadians. The Régiment de la Chaudière took Basly during the evening and then gave the advance over to 9th Canadian Infantry Brigade's North Nova Scotia Highlanders.

At Colomby, A Company, North Nova Scotia Highlanders, met some resistance as they rode towards the village on the backs of Sherbrooke Fusiliers tanks. The advance stopped while the Germans were cleared from the village. The advance then continued towards Villons-les-Buissons. Also advancing close by this route on D-Day were the infantry of 8th Canadian Infantry Brigade's Queens Own Rifles of Canada, who had made the assault on Nan White Beach earlier in the morning. They were on the left flank, making for the village of Anguerny.

DIRECTIONS: Follow the road round to the right as you enter Colomby-sur-Thaon and then turn left at the crossroads after about 300 metres, heading towards Anguerny, which was liberated by the Queen's Own Rifles in the early evening.

BATTLEFIELD TOURS

A blazing ammunition truck sends plumes of smoke skywards during the advance inland from the landings. *(Ken Bell, NAC PA-131375)*

Continue along the winding D141 road through Anguerny following the signs to Mathieu. Pass out of the village and continue along the D141, still following the signs for Mathieu. After a while the roads runs for about 1 km alongside the dual carriageway into Caen. At the roundabout take the first exit, the D220, towards Anisy and pull over by the monument just short of the village.

THE SITE: This was the limit of 8th Canadian Infantry Brigade's advance on D-Day. The Queen's Own Rifles advanced from Anguerny and captured Anisy late in the evening, digging in around here for the night. This area was the most easterly point reached by the landings from Juno Beach. Behind you, on the other side of the dual carriageway, was the Sword Beach sector of 3rd British Infantry Division. By the evening of D-Day, the nearest British troops were established at Périers-sur-le-Dan, 3 km away to the east. This left a wide gap between the British and Canadians and it was this gap that the German had exploited earlier in the day. The area near here had been the scene of great activity during the few hours before the Queen's Own Rifles had arrived for, to the south, behind the houses on the opposite side of the road, elements of 21st Panzer Division had driven north in the late afternoon during their counter-attack on the landings. The motorised infantry of 192nd Panzergrenadier Regiment had attacked towards Lion-sur-Mer from near Cambes, 2 km to the south of this point, roughly along the line of the dual carriageway behind you. Their attack failed and the panzergrenadiers were withdrawn at around 2100 hours, digging in for the night between Cambes and Epron, 3 km to the south of this point.

British military police search German prisoners beside the railway line near Bernières. *(Frank L. Dubervill, NAC PA-175957)*

DIRECTIONS: Continue straight along the D220 through the edge of Anisy and on to the crossroads with the D79. You have now arrived back on the axis of the North Nova Scotia Highlanders' advance on D-Day. The battalion came from the right along this road and then proceeded down the route ahead of you into Villons-les-Buissons.

Turn left along the D79 and after a just under 1 km turn sharp right. Immediately on the right is a monument which you may wish to stop and view. The memorial is to the Norwegians who took part in the liberation of Europe, including the Spitfire pilots of 132 (Norwegian) Wing of 84 Group, 2nd Tactical Air Force, who were stationed at the nearby B16 airfield at Villons-les-Buissons.

Continue into Villons-les-Buissons. Turn left at the junction and drive through the village on the D220. A few hundred metres outside the village, opposite the large grain store, pull over to the right by a monument alongside the road junction on your right.

THE SITE: This is the furthest point inland that Canadian troops reached on D-Day. This is the spot known as 'Hell's Corner' and the memorial relates to the hazardous nature of the locality here from 7 June to 7 July 1944. Although the Canadians advanced 4 km further south on 7 June, they were beaten back

The plaque at Villons-les-Buissons at the forward edge of 3rd Canadian Infantry Division's positions. *(Author)*

into this position by the *Hitlerjugend* Division. The front line remained here for a further 32 days, overlooked and shelled and mortared constantly by the Germans. The infantry quickly adopted the nickname Hell's Corner to describe what it was like trying to get past this point. To the left of the monument is the entrance to the Château des Buissons, a building that received much hostile German attention while the front line was so static for so long.

DIRECTIONS: Continue south on the D220 for 2 km into Buron. Go straight on at the traffic lights and pull over into the small square on the right after about 200 metres.

THE SITE: In the centre are two monuments, one to the Highland Light Infantry of Canada and the other to the Sherbrooke Fusiliers. The village was liberated on the morning of 7 June by the North Nova Scotia Highlanders and Sherbrooke Fusiliers but was lost again that afternoon to 12th SS Panzer Division. It was recaptured and then given up again that day and remained in German hands until early in July.

DIRECTIONS: Continue southwards out of the village.

THE SITE: The open ground here was the scene of much bloodshed during the German counter-attack of 7 June.

BATTLEFIELD TOURS

Present in the tank battle here on D+1 was Lieutenant Norman Davies of B Squadron, Sherbrooke Fusiliers.

'I spotted seven or eight enemy tanks at 1,000 yards on my left. I halted, stopped two of them with the 17-pdr gun, advanced, halted and fired again scoring another hit, then all hell seemed to break loose. There were tanks coming up at full speed to my rear (our own), tanks to my left firing at us, anti-tank blazing away from our left and rear, and tracer and 75-mm gun flashes all over the place. Tanks were hit and burning all around us by then, and it was impossible to keep track of who was who. One was hit directly in front of me, one right beside me. 88 tracer was cutting down trees all over the place. I decided to withdraw with what was left of 2nd and 3rd Troops. At les Buissons, we counted noses and found we had five tanks left out of the twenty that had gone in.'

Source: John Marteinson & Michael McNorgan, *The Royal Canadian Armoured Corps*, p. 243.

THIS IS THE END OF THE TOUR: Go ahead to the crossroads and turn left on to the D126 towards Caen. Continue for about 2.5 km to the roundabout. If you carry straight on at this roundabout and out through the second exit, the *Mémorial de Caen* museum lies half a kilometre ahead. This is the area of la Folie and the location of GenLt Richter's headquarters during the landings. If you take the third exit from the roundabout it will lead you, after 2 km, to the D7 and the road to Courseulles.

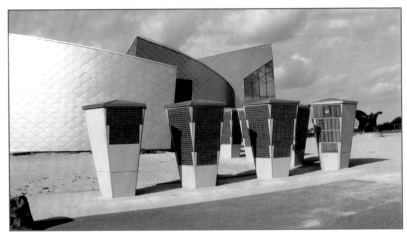

The Juno Beach Centre. *(Author)*

TOUR B

7ᵗʰ BRIGADE'S LANDINGS AND ADVANCE INLAND

OBJECTIVE: This tour starts with 7th Canadian Infantry Brigade's landings on Mike Beach and follows the route taken for part of its drive inland.

DURATION/SUITABILITY: The tour covers 24 km in all and is likely to take half a day. It is good for the cyclist, mostly over quiet country roads, with some low hills. Unfortunately it is less good for the disabled. The first part of the tour is a walking tour of Mike Beach, none of which can be viewed from a car; the whole beach is hidden behind sand dunes. Juno Centre does have disabled access, however, and all sites of the inland part of the tour can be reached by car.

DIRECTIONS: Start the tour by the DD Sherman tank near the entrance to Courseulles harbour (*described in Tour A*). Follow the road round to the south passing alongside the harbour on your right. Continue for around 300 metres and turn right over the swing bridge if it is open, if not, continue ahead and pass round the marina and up the opposite side to the junction with the swing bridge. Turn left, westwards, on to the D514 towards Arromanches. Follow the road for a few hundred metres out of Courseulles and take the next turning on the right just before the bridge, with a sign saying Juno Beach Centre. Continue across another narrow bridge and turn right on to the drive that leads up to the Juno Beach Centre. Park in the car park to visit the museum. Then walk across the grass towards the sea.

THE SITE: The Juno Beach Centre was opened in June 2003 to provide not only a history of Canada during the Second World War, but an insight into the growth and development of the nation. The exhibitions in the various galleries in the centre make good use of the latest interactive techniques, films and sound recordings. It is a thoroughly modern museum in a striking modern building.

BATTLEFIELD TOURS

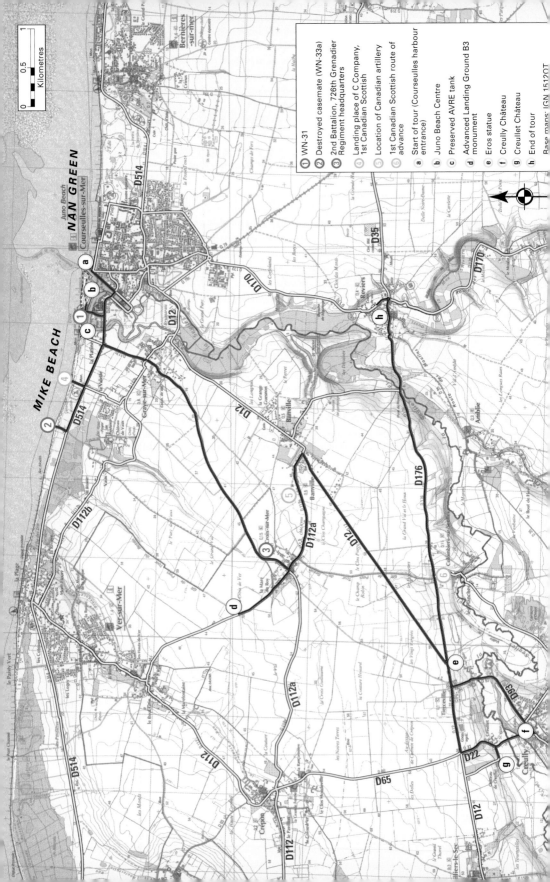

Legend

1. WN-31
2. Destroyed casemate (WN-33a)
3. 2nd Battalion, 726th Grenadier Regiment headquarters
4. Landing place of C Company, 1st Canadian Scottish
5. Location of Canadian artillery
6. 1st Canadian Scottish route of advance

a. Start of tour (Courseulles harbour entrance)
b. Juno Beach Centre
c. Preserved AVRE tank
d. Advanced Landing Ground B3 monument
e. Eros statue
f. Creully Château
g. Creullet Château
h. End of tour

Base map: IGN 1512OT

Juno Beach Centre

Juno Beach Centre, Voie des Français Libres, BP 104, 14470 Courseulles-sur-Mer; tel: +33 (0)2 31 37 32 17; web: <www.junobeach.org>; email: <contact@junobeach.org>. Open: 1000–1300 & 1400–1800 daily, Feb–Mar & Oct–Dec; 0900–1900 daily, Apr–Sept; closed Jan. Entrance fee.

You are now well within the fortified area that protected the western side of the entrance to Courseulles harbour. The dunes ahead of you mark the top of Mike Red Beach, the landing place of the assault companies of the Winnipeg Rifles. Slightly to the right is a low concrete structure with a raised mound at the far end. This is the surface of one of the defensive bunkers, which

The large concrete bunker just behind the dunes at the top of Mike Red Beach. The whole structure was built underground, with very little of it visible on the surface. To the rear is the Juno Beach Centre. *(Author)*

formed part of strongpoint WN-31. On the top of the raised concrete mound are the remains of a steel ring, which was once the base of the thick steel cupola that crowned this emplacement. The cutting and welding marks that were made to remove the steel structure for scrap after the war can be clearly seen. The cupola would have housed a machine gun with a dominating view of the beach, but the shifting sand dunes nearby have now spoilt this view.

DIRECTIONS: Walk to the right towards the harbour entrance, and then turn towards the sea.

THE SITE: Half buried in the dunes is a massive casemate, which once held a 50-mm gun sited to fire along the length of Mike Beach. Sand erosion has caused the emplacement to sink on one side and it now rests at a precarious angle. From this position you can see the whole of Mike Beach. Immediately in front of you is Mike Red sector, with Mike White and Mike Green sector stretching into the distance towards Gold Beach. About 2 km away, where the beach curves towards the sea, another gun casemate can be seen which covered the beach from a westerly

BATTLEFIELD TOURS

German 50-mm gun casemate situated on the extreme eastern edge of Mike Red Beach. Over the years the emplacement has gradually slipped into the sand through erosion and the shifting of the dunes on which it was built. *(Author)*

position. Between these two gun positions, a third casemate – located about 250 metres away by the curved grey building at the top of the beach – housed a powerful 75-mm gun. These three heavy artillery pieces, impervious to naval bombardment, were able to sweep the beach with heavy fire.

DIRECTIONS: Walk west along the top of the beach for around 150 metres and take one of the paths back towards the Juno Beach Centre. Dotted amongst the dunes are the remains of several concrete works that made up the strongpoint, including Tobruk pits which once held a machine gun or mortar.

Return to your car and follow the drive out of the Juno Centre. At the junction with the narrow bridge on the left continue westwards past the *École de Voile* and park in the small car park to the right by the top of the dunes. Leave the car and walk back along the dunes towards the sail training school to the massive German bunker that blocks your path.

THE SITE: This was the emplacement for the 75-mm gun, which had a commanding field of fire along the top of the beach. It was protected on its seaward side by a thick concrete wall making it almost invulnerable to the fire of Allied warships.

Damage to the top of the casemate does show that some heavy calibre weapon or bomb did manage to strike it, but its eventual demise was brought about by close-range gunfire from tanks that had landed on the beach. The casemate is still within the fortified zone of WN-31 and helped to guard the exit from the beach that led on to the narrow bridge behind you. It was here on the beach in front that the Winnipeg Rifles assault companies landed. The leading waves came ashore right in front of this position and had to fight their way up the beach and into the mined and wired area that made up the strongpoint. Once through this line of defence the Winnipeg Rifles moved further inland across the small bridge and on to what was an island formed by the meandering River Seulles and the entrance to the harbour.

> **Lance-Corporal John McLean of C Company, Royal Winnipeg Rifles, landed here and recalls getting into the barbed wire surrounding the strongpoint.**
>
> 'I was about half way through the wire when I was hit. The blast stunned me and I fell into the wire. I don't know if I was out for seconds or minutes. By the time I came to, the remaining survivors were through the wire and into the sand dunes. When I looked up, there were bits of bloody cloth on the wire to my right and my first thought was that maybe my legs were gone. Although I felt no pain, I looked around and found my legs still intact, but a few feet behind me, one of my comrades was minus HIS legs and was dead.'
>
> *Source*: Jean Portugal, *We Were There, The Army*, Vol 6, p. 2890.

Go back down to the bridge and look along the river bank to the right. Set up on the bank is a concrete German infantry position with two Tobruk pits on its roof. These formed part of the strongpoint and were sited to defend the inland approaches and access to the bridge. On the right of the bridge on the far side is a plaque commemorating the building of a permanent structure here after the assault by 85th Field Company, Royal Engineers, from 102nd Beach Group Sub-Area. This unit had the overall responsibility of organising Juno Beach after the attacking troops had moved on. The engineers called the bridge 'Nottingham Bridge' after the city where the field company was raised.

The double Tobruk emplacement guarding the loop in the River Seulles, west of Courseulles. The structure was built into the river bank and, with summer vegetation surrounding it, would have been almost impossible to detect. *(Author)*

DIRECTIONS: Move back over the bridge to the small car park and then continue along the top of the dunes towards the large stainless steel Cross of Lorraine ahead of you. This cross commemorates the return of General de Gaulle to French soil on 14 June 1944 after four years in exile. He landed near this spot, just to the west of where you are standing.

Carry on westward along the dunes for 100 metres past another German position with a Tobruk pit on its roof until you come to a gap leading down to the beach.

THE SITE: Stand on the highest point of the dunes alongside the path from the beach and look inland to the south. This was one of the main exits opened up by the Royal Engineers of 79th Armoured Division. The road inland from here was mined and blocked by an anti-tank ditch. The ground to the right was soft and marshy, inundated by the Germans by blocking a culvert that ran under the road. About 100 metres along the road, near the first of the houses on the left, was the ditch. It was here that an AVRE from 26th Assault Squadron came to grief whilst trying to lay a fascine across the gap. The tank slipped into the ditch and became stranded. Two of the crew escaped, but three others were killed by German fire. The tank now blocked the exit road. However, an enterprising officer sent a bridging tank forward to lay a prefabricated bridge across the ditch, placing it on top of the stranded AVRE, thus opening the road for traffic. As the day wore on and more and more vehicles moved over the bridge, it began to subside. Other engineers came forward and bulldozed rubble into the gap to fill the void, completely burying the AVRE. There the tank remained for more than 30 years until rescued by French civilians assisted by modern-day Royal Engineers. The tank was then restored to its wartime condition and returned to the scene. It now rests just below you at the back of Mike Beach, forming a memorial to the men of 79th Armoured Division who lost their lives during the liberation of Europe.

This sector of Juno Beach was not only the landing place of General de Gaulle, but also that of General Montgomery when he came to France. It also saw the arrival of Winston Churchill and King George VI when they visited Normandy a few days after the landings. They left the beach by this exit and took the road inland through Graye-sur-Mer to Monty's HQ near Creully.

The great Cross of Lorraine above the dunes at the rear of Mike Red Beach. In the foreground is a German personnel bunker now used as a café. *(Author)*

DIRECTIONS: Having inspected the Churchill AVRE, return to your car by the road at the back of the dunes, past a German blockhouse now converted into a café. Motor over the narrow bridge that you came in by to rejoin the main road out of Courseulles. Turn right and continue to the second set of traffic lights a few hundred metres further on. Turn right towards the beach. Park and walk through the dunes down to the shore.

The track leading from Mike Beach inland through the dunes towards Graye-sur-Mer was the first exit from the landings to be opened and it was made possible by bridging a broken culvert using a stranded AVRE as part of the foundations. The crossing place was located alongside the first white house to the left of the track. The submerged tank was recovered in 1976, refurbished and put on display here. It can be seen in the foreground of the picture and on page 1. *(Author)*

THE SITE: This is Mike Green sector on the extreme western side of Juno Beach. It was here that C Company of 1st Battalion, Canadian Scottish, landed on D-Day. The company was attached to the Winnipeg Rifles for the assault and had the role of protecting the right flank of the Canadian landings. Its first task was to eliminate the large gun casemate to the west, which can be seen jutting out on to the beach 500 metres away. C Company, Canadian Scottish, had a relatively quiet landing as most of the opposition was centred upon the strongpoint further to the east.

DIRECTIONS: Go back to the junction with the main road.

THE SITE: To the left of the traffic lights is a memorial to the Inns of Court Regiment, which landed on the beach behind you and exited along this road. This armoured car regiment had the special task of advancing rapidly inland into the rear of the enemy, avoiding all possible resistance to make for the bridges over the River Orne up to 40 km to the south. Here the reconnaissance troops and their supporting engineers were to carry out bridge demolitions along the river in order to help isolate the landings from any German reinforcements that might be brought forward. The regiment was unfortunate to lose some of its armoured cars during the landings and then suffered serious delays in getting others off the beach. It was not successful in any of its objectives.

DIRECTIONS: Turn right at the traffic lights and continue westwards for around 800 metres and then turn right into a narrow road leading to the beach, sign-posted Brèche le Bisson. Park at the end and walk to the shore.

THE SITE: This point is near the junction of Gold and Juno Beaches. 50th (Northumbrian) Division landed on Gold Beach at la Rivière, which can be seen about 1 km away to the west. A very short distance along the dunes to the east is the large casemate that was the target of C Company, 1st Canadian Scottish. The bunker had apertures on both sides allowing the gun inside to bring fire down on both Gold and Juno Beaches. Thick concrete protected its seaward face. When the infantry reached the emplacement to eliminate the weapon and its crew,

The 75-mm casemate near the junction of Mike and Love Beaches to the west of Courseulles. This emplacement was one of the first objectives of C Company, 1st Canadian Scottish, who landed at H-Hour with the Winnipeg Rifles. When the troops arrived at the bunker they found that it had already been destroyed by naval bombardment. *(Author)*

they found that the job had already been done for them by naval gunfire. This is particularly interesting, for almost every report made by the assaulting infantry and by experts after D-Day relates how ineffective the pre-invasion bombardment and bombing were in their attempts to destroy concrete bunkers. Most were neutralised by infantry or tanks at close quarters. This example is different; it is on a slight headland and this enabled a warship, far away to the east near St-Aubin, to bring shellfire on to its weaker flanks. The damage done by the large calibre weapons and subsequent demolition by Royal Engineers can be clearly seen.

DIRECTIONS: Return to your car, drive back to the main road and turn left towards Courseulles. Continue to the second set of traffic lights and turn right towards Graye-sur-Mer.

THE SITE: This was the route taken by A Company, Winnipeg Rifles, after it had come ashore behind the assault waves on Mike Red Beach. The Winnipeg Rifles swept through the village and continued on towards Ste-Croix and Banville. The rising ground that can be seen behind the village gave a good view of the beach to the German infantry emplaced there. Several of the assault companies which landed on Mike Beach complained of persistent small arms fire coming from this high ground and interfering with the initial moves inland.

SS-Obersturmführer (Lieutenant) Peter Hansmann of the Armoured Car Company of 12th SS Panzer Division had been roused from his bed at 0230 hours on 6 June and told to carry out a reconnaissance of the eastern coastal sector near Courseulles. Soon after dawn he dismounted from his eight-wheeled armoured car and watched the landings from this high ground behind Gold and Juno Beaches.

'The enemy advance groups were not far from the coastal road. They were forming up and I was contemplating if and how we could cut off an advance group or a scouting party, and grab them. In the middle of these thoughts dropped a bad surprise from the sky. Suddenly, the ground around us was shaking, almost without warning. There had only been the slurping sound dropping bombs make, but we had not noticed any aircraft. Then it came to me, this was ship's artillery. There were immense explosions, whole mountains of dirt were hurled into the air and came crashing down in a radius of a few hundred metres. We were pressed flat to the ground wishing to be back in our steel hulls which would at least protect us from shrapnel. The 8-wheeler was waving back and forth, chunks of earth were crashing into the armour. As long as we could hear that everything was all right, we would not hear a direct hit at all.'

Source: Hubert Meyer, *The History of the 12. SS Panzer-division 'Hitlerjugend'*, p. 30.

Canadian infantry in slit trenches looking out towards enemy positions during the fighting following the landings. *(Ken Bell, NAC PA-129043)*

DIRECTIONS: At the entrance to Graye-sur-Mer turn left at the junction and then take the next road on the right after a few metres, heading towards Ste-Croix. Follow the road out of the village and after about 1 km bear to the right at a fork. Continue for 2 km more until you reach the outskirts of Ste-Croix-sur-Mer.

THE SITE: It was here on the northern edge of Ste-Croix that *Major* Lehmann, commander of 2nd Battalion, 726th Grenadier Regiment, had his headquarters. Lehmann led his men out across the open ground you have crossed during several counter-attacks against the advancing Winnipeg Rifles but they were continually forced back by the supporting Canadian armour. The 1st Hussars tanks overwhelmed the German infantry, who lacked any anti-tank capability other than hand-held panzerfausts and anti-tank mines. GenLt Richter, commander of 716th Infantry Division, attempted to reinforce Lehmann's exposed battalion with anti-tank guns from 21st Panzer Division's 200th Tank Hunter Battalion, but they never arrived. Lehmann's troops continued fighting in the village throughout the morning and into the afternoon. C Company, Winnipeg Rifles, was joined in the late morning by 7th Canadian Infantry Brigade's follow-up battalion, 1st Canadian Scottish, who pressed home the attack. Eventually the command post was surrounded and overrun, with Lehmann dying a hero's death according to a report by Richter. The Canadian Scottish then set about clearing the village of snipers and other pockets of resistance. A small group of Germans, led by their adjutant, managed to evade capture until nightfall, when they made their escape back to the German lines.

DIRECTIONS: Continue into the village to the road junction opposite the church where a plaque on the wall of the churchyard commemorates the Canadians lost in taking the village. Turn right and follow the road to Ver-sur-Mer. After 1 km on the right is a memorial surrounded by a low stone wall.

Monument marking the location of Airfield B3 to the west of Ste-Croix. The main runway ran across the field in the background. This was the first British airfield in Normandy to become operational when fighters landed on 11 June. (*Author*)

THE SITE: Several tablets recall Advanced Landing Ground B3, which was constructed in this area immediately after the landings. RAF Servicing Commandos landed with the follow-up waves on Juno Beach on 6 June and made their way immediately to this point to begin preparing an airfield for Allied fighters. The smooth open arable land on this long plateau was perfect for landing aircraft and a runway was made by laying rolls of steel mesh to bind the dirt surface together – a piece of this steel matting can be seen in front of the memorial. The airfield became operational on 11 June, ready to receive fighter aircraft from England, the first British landing ground in Normandy to do so. The main 1,700-metre runway crossed the road just ahead of the memorial. The airfield was in use until mid-September 1944.

DIRECTIONS: Turn around and retrace the route back into Ste-Croix. Continue through the village past the church along the D112a to Banville. The area on the left was the position of 3rd Canadian Infantry Division's 12th and 13th Field Regiments on 6 June. They moved onto the open hills here during the late morning and early afternoon to support the advancing infantry with their 105-mm Priest self-propelled guns. Continue into the centre of Banville and give way at the road junction. Turn right on to the D12 heading towards Bayeux. Continue 3 km to the roundabout, take the first exit and pull over where safe.

In the centre of the roundabout behind you is a tall column supporting a statue of the god Eros. It was made by 179th Field Company, RE, from concrete and iron and was erected on the roundabout in August 1944 as a copy of the statue in Piccadilly Circus in London.

Continue along the D12 into Tierceville and take the next turning on the left towards Creully, the D93. Motor down to the bridge over the River Seulles on the southern side of Tierceville.

THE SITE: A Company, Winnipeg Rifles, took this route from Mike Beach, crossing the river here and then moving on into Creully. The town marked the inland boundary between the landings on Gold and Juno Beaches. Creully was liberated during the afternoon of D-Day by 7th Battalion, The Green Howards, supported by the tanks of 4th/7th Royal Dragoon Guards, both of 50th (Northumbrian) Division. The Canadians made contact with the British here and thus linked together the two landings.

DIRECTIONS: Continue into Creully along its main street and then take the right hand turning just after the church. A short distance along on the right is an impressive memorial to 4th/7th Dragoon Guards. Towering alongside on the right hand side of the monument is the château of Creully. This building is often mistakenly identified as being the location of Montgomery's HQ in Normandy, but the actual location of his command post was in fact just north of the river at Creullet, 500 metres away. Continue over the bridge and, as the road sweeps round to the right, turn left into the lay-by on the opposite side of the road.

Château de Creullet, General Montgomery's HQ in Normandy. It was from here that he directed the battle in the first few weeks after the landings. *(Author)*

THE SITE: Montgomery's headquarters was located in the château up the lane to your left. As the lane becomes one-way for traffic a little distance along, a short walk up this lane will bring you to the gates of the Château de Creullet. There is a plaque alongside the gateway in French commemorating Monty's tenure of the building and the visit of General de Gaulle. It was here in the grounds of the château that Monty received all of his important visitors, briefed the media and carried out numerous investitures and ceremonies during the fighting in Normandy.

DIRECTIONS: Return to your car and carry on along the D22 away from Creully up to the junction with the D12. Turn right and continue to the roundabout. Take the first exit along the D176 towards Reviers. After about 1 km there is a crossroads with the road into Colombiers-sur-Seulles on the right.

THE SITE: This road to the right was the route taken by 1st Canadian Scottish on their drive inland after the landings on Mike Beach. The battalion went on to liberate Colombiers, Pierrepont and Cainet before the end of the day. It was also the path taken by the Winnipeg Rifles on the continuation of its move inland. The next day the Winnipegs resumed 7th Brigade's advance through Secqueville-en-Bessin and moved on to cross over the Caen–Bayeux road to Putot-en-Bessin thus becoming the first Canadian unit to reach its D-Day objective.

THIS IS THE END OF THE TOUR: Continue towards Reviers, over the Seulles again, and into the village. At the round-about take the third exit to return to Courseulles by the D170.

TOUR C

NAN BEACH AND 48 RM COMMANDO

OBJECTIVE: This tour explores the landings over the Nan sector of Juno Beach and follows 48 Royal Marine Commando's path to its D-Day objective in Langrune-sur-Mer.

DURATION/SUITABILITY: The tour covers some 10 km and is likely to take half a day to complete. It is excellent for the cyclist with the whole tour being made along flat seafront roads and cycle paths. It is also good for the disabled, but the first part of the tour does involves walking along the (flat) promenade.

DIRECTIONS: Start the tour by the DD tank by the harbour in Courseulles (*see Tour A*). Follow the road behind the beach eastwards, away from the harbour entrance. Turn right at the end and go on to the traffic lights. Turn left on to the D514 towards Ouistreham. Continue to Bernières following the road round several bends to a set of traffic lights. Go straight on at the lights and turn left after 100 metres into a parking area just behind the beach. This is the Place de 6 Juin. Walk towards the beach.

NAN GREEN

Juno Beach

Courseulles-sur-Mer

NAN WHITE

NAN RED

St-Aubin-sur-Mer

Bernières-sur-mer

Langrune-sur-Mer

Luc-sur-Mer

Taillevile

la Délivrande

① WN-28
② WN-27
③ WN-26
④ A Company, Queen's Own Rifles' landing place
⑤ 48 RM Commando's route of advance
⑥ Point at which 48 RM Commando's advance split up
⑦ Rendezvous point with Sword Beach
a   Start of tour (Courseulles harbour entrance)
b   Place de 6 Juin
c   Hôtel de la Plage
d   Manoir des Templiers
e   End of tour (Luc-sur-Mer No. 1 Commando Memorial)

Kilometres
0   0.5   1

Troops from 9th Canadian Infantry Brigade land from LCI(L)s west of Bernières during the early afternoon of D-Day. *(Gilbert Alexander Milne, NAC PA-145349)*

THE SITE: On the right is a large Norman house that features prominently in many of the pictures of the D-Day landings at Bernières. Stop by the memorial on the promenade, which remembers the heroes who made the landings and paid the ultimate sacrifice. You are now at the top of Nan White Beach opposite the landing place of the Queen's Own Rifles of Canada.

DIRECTIONS: Turn left and walk westwards along the promenade to the end of the row of buildings. On the left is the Life Saving Station (*Station de Sauvetage*) with a plaque on the wall to the North Nova Scotia Highlanders who landed here with the follow-up 9th Canadian Infantry Brigade. Walk on past a row of bathing huts to the open dunes.

THE SITE: This is the area of the beach where A Company, Queen's Own Rifles, landed on D-Day. The men of the company landed half way between low and high tide and had to cross over 200 metres of open beach before they reached the wire entanglements barring the way on to the dunes behind you. Well-camouflaged machine guns and mortars in the sandy hillocks along the shoreline raked the area with deadly fire. The

The ground behind the western sector of Nan White Beach. The railway from Courseulles ran across the foreground of the picture. The village of Bernières is to the left and Courseulles is 2 km to the right. *(Author)*

countryside inland behind the dunes remains as it was in 1944. The Canadian assault troops moved over this ground and the railway line from Courseulles, which cut across this area, to get to the western side of Bernières. While crossing this open space they were caught in a minefield and then picked off by machine-gun and mortar fire, taking heavy casualties.

Sergeant Charles Cromwell Martin, A Company, Queen's Own Rifles, crossed the dunes at this point on D-Day.

'Once over the railway we had some grass cover but we ran into heavy barbed wire. We had to decide whether to cut the wire here and move straight ahead to the houses two hundred yards away, or cut the wire to the left or the right and move in that direction. We decided to go straight ahead. I cut the strands and bent them back, making an opening just wide enough for a man to belly through. The grass gave us some cover. The enemy knew we were somewhere and likely on the move, but they could not pinpoint us. We crept through. By this time there were about fifteen of us. Then we came to a minefield. I advanced about ten paces and stepped on a jumping mine.'

Source: Charles Martin, *Battle Diary*, p. 8.

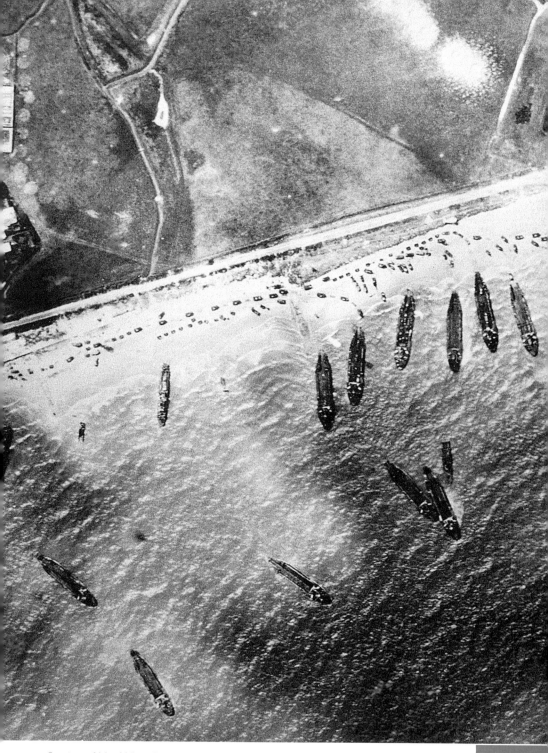

Section of Nan White Beach west of Bernières, landing place of A Company, Queen's Own Rifles. The photograph was taken during the late morning of D-Day. Vehicles of the follow-up brigade are beginning to clog up the narrow beach. (US National Archives)

Machine-gun post at the top of Nan White Beach close by the junction with Nan Red Beach. The sea wall that runs through the centre of the picture was 3 metres high on D-Day and was topped by barbed wire. The wall and this position would have overlooked the Canadian infantry as they rushed across the beach from their landing craft. *(Author)*

DIRECTIONS: Turn around and go back to the monument by the Place de 6 Juin. Continue a few steps eastwards and immediately on the right is the large Norman house with a plaque outside. This is the 'Maison de le Queen's Own Rifles of Canada', one of the first houses to be liberated on D-Day. It is prominent in most of the photographs taken of the landings at Bernières. The plaque outside gives details of the landings here. Continue eastwards along the promenade.

THE SITE: After a short distance you come to the area of the strongpoint WN-28, which covered this stretch of the shore. The fortified area was based around the slight prominence ahead of you that juts out on to the sands, sited to give it a commanding view along Nan White Beach. All of the inland features have now disappeared, but a number of concrete structures built into the sea wall here have survived. The first is a filled-in Tobruk mortar pit that juts out from the promenade. In 1944 the sea wall here stood about 3 metres above the beach and was topped with barbed wire. This Tobruk emplacement would have towered

Mortar pit built against the sea wall on Nan White Beach, now a memorial to the Queen's Own Rifles. *(Author)*

above the infantry and its mortar would have pummelled the sands with fire. B Company, Queen's Own Rifles, came ashore in front of this position and a plaque on the seaward side of the pit commemorates this.

Fifty metres further on is a gun emplacement which housed a 50-mm anti-tank gun. Stand inside the casemate and look back westwards along the beach. You can clearly see the strength of this position. Its gun had a maximum range of 6,500 metres and could fire along the whole shoreline all the way to Nan Green Beach at Courseulles. The seaward side of the emplacement is protected by thick concrete making it impervious to naval gunfire. The first tank landing craft and armoured vehicles landing on this beach were all vulnerable to fire from this gun. Behind the gun position, following the sea wall around to the east, are two other weapons pits built into the sea wall.

The area here is now called le Place de Canada and the walls of the former German positions are topped with commemorative plaques to the various units which landed here, including memorials to the Queen's Own Rifles, Fort Garry Horse, Régiment de la Chaudière, and 5th Battalion, Royal Berkshire Regiment. The Berkshire battalion was the infantry component of the beach group; its task was to clear any German stragglers

The inside of the 50-mm gun emplacement in WN-28 at the top of the beach at Bernières. *(Author)*

and provide organisation and security for the landing of the follow-up waves. Nearby is an orientation table showing details of the landings and also of the Canadian move inland.

When B Company, Queen's Own Rifles, hit the beach during the assault phase, the tide was coming in but there was still over 200 metres of open sand to be crossed in the face of withering

BATTLEFIELD TOURS

fire from this strongpoint before any cover could be had. Even then the only shelter was along the sea wall underneath the guns of the resistance post. These seafront emplacements and the trenches and weapons pits behind them, stretching back inland almost 100 metres to the railway line, had to be taken by hand-to-hand fighting. Tank support from the DD tanks and the specialised armour was slow in arriving and B Company suffered 65 casualties in trying to subdue this position.

Ahead along the promenade you are looking towards Nan Red Beach and the landing point of the North Shore Regiment.

Return along the promenade to the Place de 6 Juin. This area was the main exit from Nan White Beach and led directly into the town. It was through this square that Maj-Gen Keller, commander of 3rd Canadian Infantry Division, came ashore during the late morning of 6 June (*see picture on p. 99*).

Leave the car park and cross the main road, then walk a short way down Rue de le Régiment de la Chaudière towards the centre of Bernières. House number 288 on the left was once the *Hôtel de la Plage* and was commandeered for a short while on the morning of D-Day as Maj-Gen Keller's forward command post. It later became the base for war correspondents covering the landings. A plaque commemorates these events.

DIRECTIONS: Return to the main road, cross to the Place de 6 Juin, then walk a short distance east towards Ouistreham. On the left is the old train station of Bernières, now the tourist office. The rail line here ran along the route now used by the D514 to Ouistreham. On the other side of the road is the position of the deep anti-tank ditch barring the route inland from the beaches.

DIRECTIONS: Return to your car. Turn left out of the car park on to the D514 towards Ouistreham. After about 1 km, just as the road bends to the right by a large island in the middle of the road, turn left towards St-Aubin along the continuation of the D514. Proceed for 500 metres to a grassy area on the left, pull over and park. You have now reached Nan Red Beach. Walk a little way to the right and then down the short ramp to the beach.

THE SITE: This stretch of Nan Red Beach sits in a curve of the shoreline, with Bernières to the west and St-Aubin about 600 metres to the east. It was here that B Company, North Shore

9th Canadian Infantry Brigade lands over Nan White Beach at Bernières during the late morning of D-Day. The width of the beach has been reduced to just a few metres by the incoming tide and the small stretch of dry sand at the top is becoming congested by troops and equipment, slowing up the arrival of the follow-up battalions. *(IWM A23938)*

Regiment, landed during the assault waves; A Company landed further to the west and moved inland to clear the eastern part of Bernières, which it did with relatively light casualties. B Company came ashore into very heavy fire from the strongpoint at St-Aubin. It landed in front of the point where you are now standing. On D-Day this particular area was the site of a large house with a walled garden. The seaward side of its perimeter formed a high sea wall, which jutted out on to the beach. On either side of this sea wall, the top of the beach was flanked by sand dunes to the west and sandy cliffs to the east. The men of the North Shore Regiment immediately made for the cover of this wall and the shelter of the cliffs. Here they were away from the worst of the fire sweeping the beach, but were vulnerable to the plunging fire of mortars. B Company eventually exited the beach through the open area to the west, through wired obstacles and a minefield, then turned eastwards along the lateral road behind you to attack strongpoint WN-27 in St-Aubin, the source of most of the interdictory fire that was sweeping the beach.

Nan Red Beach just to the east of Bernières. B Company, North Shore Regiment, landed near the bottom of the picture, in front of the large house on the beach with a high sea wall. A Company landed to the right, opposite the seaside villas. The ground at the rear of the beach has been pockmarked by hundreds of 5-inch rockets fired from the LCT(R)s which accompanied the assault landing craft. *(IWM MH24332)*

Landing 30 minutes behind the assault waves was 48 RM Commando. The six landing craft infantry carrying Lt-Col Moulton's Royal Marines came in to this stretch of the beach, using the large house where you are standing as their aiming point. Moulton's boat landed on the beach in front, with the other five craft off to the right. Two craft on the extreme right became snared on underwater obstacles and began sinking, swept all the time by fire from WN-27. Many men of Y and Z Troops who took to the water were swept away and drowned. The troops from the other craft ran into an even fiercer fire than that which had caught the North Shore Regiment. The strongpoint at St-Aubin was at that moment under attack by the Canadians of B Company, but it was still able to bring down heavy fire on the beach. The marines all sought shelter beneath the sea wall and the sandy cliffs. Here they were pinned down, their numbers being whittled away by mortar and machine-gun fire, until Moulton organised them and led them from the beach.

> **Marine Jock Mathieson was amongst the commandos taking cover behind the wall that day.**
>
> 'I was sheltering beside the sea wall along with others from HQ troop. Also there were many of the wounded who had crawled up the sand to find protection from the enemy fire. By that time the tide was well in and the beach was very narrow. Then a Canadian tank came forward and began running along by the wall trying to get off of the beach. The driver could not see the men on the ground because all of the tank's crew were battened down inside away from German sniper fire. Nothing could stop the great vehicle and it began to run along the base of the wall, over the wounded men stretched out on the sand. Major Dan Flunder banged on the side but got no response from the tank's crew so he slipped a mine in the path of the tank and blew its track off. It was a terrible sight to see those poor helpless men crushed in this way.'
>
> *Source*: Ken Ford, *D-Day Commando*, p. 52.

The commando moved off through an exit cleared by the engineers about 80 metres west of where you are standing, crossed the D514 and formed up in a field. Here Lt-Col Moulton discovered that 40 per cent of his men were missing.

Then: The beach at St-Aubin, seen from the 50-mm gun emplacement within strongpoint WN-27. A P-47 Thunderbolt fighter has crash-landed on the sand and a stranded DD tank can be seen in the background. *(US National Archives)*

Now: The beach at St-Aubin today, taken from the 50-mm gun emplacement of strongpoint WN-27, captured by the North Shore Regiment on D-Day. *(Author)*

The beach was a killing ground, not only of the Royal Marine commandos and the North Shore Regiment infantry, but also the naval personnel from damaged craft, beach group infantry, engineers and the crews of tanks disabled and destroyed by the active defences in St-Aubin. The sand along the line of the sea wall was a mass of bodies. Every year on 6 June, this part of the beach becomes a place of commemoration when veterans of 48 RM Commando gather to carry out a short service of remembrance for those who died. It is a very moving ceremony.

DIRECTIONS: Return to your car and continue along the D514 towards St-Aubin. After a few hundred metres, just before you are forced to turn right by a one-way system, pull over to one of the parking spaces on the left of the road.

6 June 2002; veterans of 48 RM Commando gather on Nan Red Beach to remember their dead. The ceremony is taking place on the site of the sea wall where so many young commandos were killed during the landings. *(Author)*

THE SITE: You have arrived in the centre of the St-Aubin strongpoint WN-27. The area between the road and the sea is now open, but once contained a number of buildings and weapons posts. You are on the top of the low sandy cliffs that line the shore. The siting of guns in this elevated position enabled them to bring heavy fire down on to Nan Red Beach. The road you have come up was closed by pill-boxes, wire and mines, barring the direct route into the strongpoint. The North Shore Regiment finally took the fortified position late in the morning, supported by DD tanks and AVREs, with a two-pronged assault up this road and along the road that leads from the town to the sea, 50 metres behind you. A short distance to the east by the side of the road is a German gun position. This still contains the 50-mm gun covering the road up to the strongpoint. The design of the emplacement also enabled it to fire in the other direction to

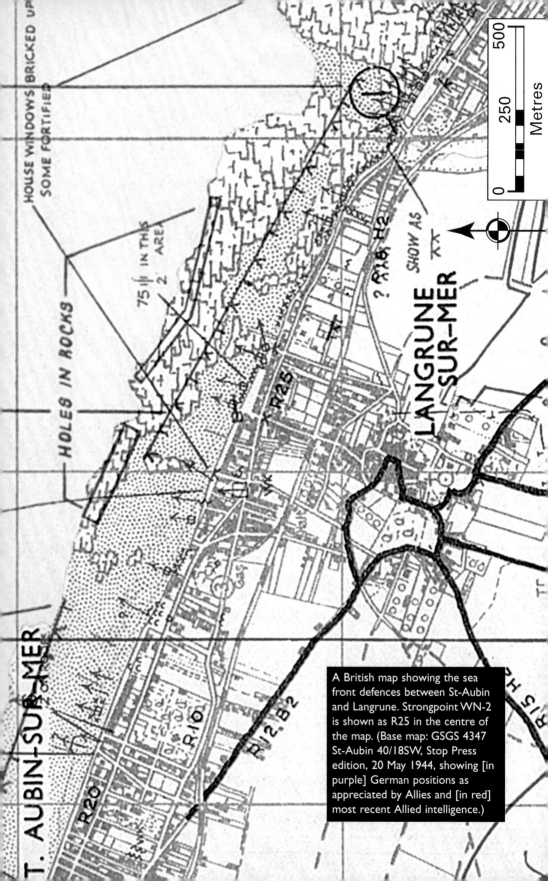

ST. AUBIN-SUR-MER

LANGRUNE SUR-MER

HOUSE WINDOWS BRICKED UP
SOME FORTIFIED

HOLES IN ROCKS

75 ₥ IN THIS
AREA 2

? R26 H2

SHOW AS ××

R25

R25

R20

R10

R12 B2

R15 H

Metres

0   250   500

A British map showing the sea
front defences between St-Aubin
and Langrune. Strongpoint WN-2
is shown as R25 in the centre of
the map. (Base map: GSGS 4347
St-Aubin 40/18SW, Stop Press
edition, 20 May 1944, showing [in
purple] German positions as
appreciated by Allies and [in red]
most recent Allied intelligence.)

the east along the seafront of St-Aubin. As elsewhere, the position is well protected on its seaward side, safe from naval gunfire. The gun remained firing until taken by the North Shore Regiment late on the morning of D-Day. To the left of the gun is a memorial to both the North Shore Regiment and 48 RM Commando. To the right, 100 metres further along, is a memorial to the Fort Garry Horse whose DD tanks landed on Nan Red and White Beaches.

DIRECTIONS: Return to your car and continue past the gun emplacement. After 50 metres you have to follow the road around to the right as part of a one-way system. This is the road up which B Company, North Shore Regiment, supported by the Fort Garry Horse Shermans, closed on the strongpoint (*see picture on p. 49*). Continue to the end of the road and turn left to pass through St-Aubin. After gathering his depleted force at the rendezvous point, Lt-Col Moulton led his commandos along this road from the right through the narrow inland streets of St-Aubin while the strongpoint on the seafront behind you was still active.

Continue through the town for about 1 km to the roundabout. It was here that Lt-Col Moulton split his commando and sent two troops to the left to clear the seafront and advance on WN-26 in Langrune from the west, while he took the remainder of his men along the inland road to the centre of the town.

Take the second exit from the roundabout and continue on the D7 towards the church in Langrune. Moulton left a troop around the church to anchor his south flank and then sent the other two troops down towards the east end of WN-26 on the seafront.

Manoir des Templiers, the D-Day headquarters of Lt-Col Moulton's 48 RM Commando during the attack on WN-26 at Langrune. (*Author*)

Continue past the church until the road curves to the right and then turn left on this bend. Once off the main road turn right immediately on the D84 towards Luc-sur-Mer. On the right is a high stone wall which flanks the Manoir des Templiers and a few metres along is the entrance to its courtyard. Lt-Col Moulton made this complex of buildings his HQ during his attack on

Langrune. Continue into open country for about 1 km until arriving at some houses by a very small bridge over a little stream.

THE SITE: The first large house on the left here at Petit Enfer became the easternmost outpost of Juno Beach on D-Day and was the point where Lieutenant John Square and a group of 48 RM Commando hoped to join up with 41 RM Commando coming from Sword Beach. The link never happened, for 41 Commando was stalled at a strongpoint in Lion-sur-Mer some 3 km away.

DIRECTIONS: Turn around and go back along the D84. Turn right just after you pass the Manoir des Templiers. You are now moving down towards the seafront along the route taken by Moulton and his men towards the strongpoint. Continue along the straight road towards the sea. Turn left at the end of the road and then park in one of the parking spaces on the right.

THE SITE: You have now arrived at the site of strongpoint WN-26 in Langrune. This large open area between the road and the sea marked the extent of the strongpoint. The road here was once lined with buildings backing on to the promenade along the seafront. The houses stretched from the road junction behind you to the traffic lights ahead of you and had their windows stopped up and their walls reinforced to form a solid block. In the middle of the road at the junctions at either end of the strongpoint were half-buried machine-gun pits, linked into the heart of WN-26 by tunnels. Along the seafront were more fortifications consisting of trenches, mortar pits, machine-gun posts and two large concrete bunkers, one containing a 50-mm anti-tank gun and one housing a 75-mm gun, sited to sweep the shoreline in either direction. Other tunnels linked the strongpoint to houses across the road to enable snipers to get in and out of the fortifications unmolested. Minefields and wire stretched for a number of metres inland along all approach roads giving further depth to the defensive position. This was one of the toughest positions along the whole of the coastline, one that had withstood heavy and constant shell-fire from warships without showing any sign of surrender. On the afternoon of D-Day 48 RM Commando attacked the strongpoint with rifles, machine guns and mortars. Unsurprisingly, it was unable to make any progress until joined by Royal Marine Centaur tanks and Canadian self-propelled anti-tank guns.

Lt-Col Moulton watches as a Canadian Wolverine tank buster moves past a knocked-out Centaur tank towards the strongpoint at Langrune. The house in the background formed part of the fortified position and was located alongside the high concrete wall which blocked entry into the compound. *(IWM B5148)*

DIRECTIONS: Walk back to the junction of the Rue de Colonel Harivel and Rue Général Leclerc which you just emerged from.

THE SITE: In 1944 there was a machine-gun post in the centre of the road and a few metres down the road towards the sea was a high concrete wall barring access into the strongpoint. This was the site of the commandos' entry into WN-26. Now turn right and walk about 100 metres along the Rue de Colonel Harivel back towards Moulton's HQ and stop. You are now roughly at the point from which the picture above was taken. The house with the balcony, just in front of Lt-Col Moulton in the picture, can be seen on the left. The tank is getting into position to bombard the concrete wall.

DIRECTIONS: Walk back to the road junction, cross over, and then walk a few metres down the slip road leading to the beach.

THE SITE: This was the location of a high concrete wall through which the tanks and commandos forced an entry into the fortifications on 7 June. The marines were then able to move through the buildings and gardens, clearing the weapons pits and trenches with sub-machine guns and grenades. Thirty-one prisoners were taken and many others were killed. Continue to the seafront. The junction of the promenade and the slip road was the site of the 75-mm gun emplacement. Turn left and walk along to the memorial on the left in the square that backs on to the sea. This commemorates the taking of WN-26 by 48 RM Commando and remembers those who died during the battle.

DIRECTIONS: Walk to the traffic lights on the right and go into the town along the Rue de la Mer. Continue to the junction about 300 metres ahead. On the left is a plaque commemorating those who died during the attack. Return to your car and drive eastwards towards Luc-sur-Mer for around 1 km. The seafront at Luc-sur-Mer contained another strongpoint, WN-25, located about 200 metres east of the casino. It was attacked and taken by 46 RM Commando, which landed over Juno Beach, on 7 June.

Pull over at this point in front of a memorial on the left.

Tobruk weapons bunker built into the sea wall at Luc-sur-Mer close by the junction of Sword and Juno Beaches. *(Author)*

THE SITE: This memorial commemorates a landing made almost three years before D-Day when No. 1 Commando raided this beach during the night of 28–29 September 1941. A Tobruk weapons pit, all that now remains of strongpoint WN-25, can be found 300 metres along the promenade to the east.

THIS IS THE END OF THE TOUR: To return to the start, turn around and drive west along the D514 out of Luc-sur-Mer, through Langrune, St-Aubin and Bernières to Courseulles.

TOUR D

SAINT-AUBIN TO DOUVRES RADAR STATION

OBJECTIVE: This tour follows the North Shore Regiment from St-Aubin, through Tailleville to the radar station near Douvres.

DURATION/SUITABILITY: The tour covers some 17 km and is likely to take about half a day. It is good for the cyclist, mostly on quiet roads with minor hills. For the disabled it is also good, but involves some walking. Disabled access is only possible to the surface area of the radar station.

DIRECTIONS: Start the tour by the DD tank in Courseulles (*see Tour A*). Follow the road behind the beach east, away from the harbour. Turn right at the end and go on to the traffic lights. Turn left on to the D514 towards Ouistreham. Continue to Bernières following the road round several bends and through a set of traffic lights. About 1 km further on the road bends to the right after the turning on the left to St-Aubin. From here the road becomes the D7b and follows the route of the old rail line which ran along the Bernières seafront then swung inland. Continue

The approach to Tailleville from St-Aubin. The North Shore Regiment attacked across this open ground on D-Day, towards the stone wall surrounding the château. *(Author)*

BATTLEFIELD TOURS

Juno Beach

Courseulles-sur-Mer

NAN GREEN

NAN WHITE

la Rive Plage

NAN RED

St-Aubin-sur-Mer

D514

D7b

Bernières-sur-mer

①

D219

Langrune-sur-Mer

D170

b

c

Taillville

D35

Reviers

D35

D79a

D35

D79

D404

③

D219

Douvres-la-Délivrande

④

②

⑤

Bény-sur-Mer

D219

d

D79

D83

Basly

D404

D7

Colomby-sur-Thaon

Anguerny

D14

① The North Shore Regiment's
   start line for advance to Tailleville

② Starting point for 17 June attack on
   Douvres Radar Station (south)

③ German-held wood

④ Douvres Radar Station (north)

⑤ Douvres Radar Station (south)

a Start of tour (Courseulles harbour
   entrance)

b Tailleville Château

c La Ferme du Prieuré

d End of tour (Douvres la Délivrande
   War Cemetery)

Base map: IGN 1612OT

0   0.5   1
Kilometres

through a short stretch of open country to a roundabout. Take the first exit (D219) towards Tailleville and pull over where safe.

THE SITE: You are now on the southern edge of St-Aubin. The North Shore Regiment's assault companies landed on Nan Red Beach on 6 June. A Company moved westwards and cleared the outskirts of Bernières, while B Company attacked WN-27 on the seafront at St-Aubin (*see Tour* C). D Company then landed and moved to the area you are now in, clearing the streets as it went. Its men established a firm base near the church behind you and sent a party to capture the area around the station, 300 metres east. Once this southern area of St-Aubin had been consolidated, C Company then came through and began the battalion's advance inland, with its first objective being the capture of the village of Tailleville which lies 2.5 km ahead of you to the south.

DIRECTIONS: Continue for about 2 km then pull off on to a farm track on the right about 500 metres short of the village.

A mortar pit which was part of the defences of Tailleville. On the extreme left is the spire of the church at St-Aubin. The trees on the right by the water tower held a German outpost, silenced by mortar fire during the attack. *(Author)*

THE SITE: Ahead of you is Tailleville with the château, surrounded by a high stone wall, being its most prominent feature. The château was the headquarters of *Hauptmann* (Captain) Deptolla, commander of 2nd Battalion, 736th Grenadier Regiment. The headquarters and the village were

BATTLEFIELD TOURS

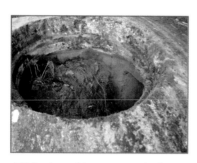

A Tobruk machine-gun post built against the wall surrounding the château at Tailleville. The entrance at the rear of the post led through the wall into the château's grounds, providing an easy escape route for the defenders. *(Author)*

garrisoned by 8th Company, 736th Grenadier Regiment, commanded by *Hauptmann* Johann Grzeski. On D-Day, this was the open ground over which the North Shore Regiment advanced to capture the village. What the North Shore men did not realise was that this village was a veritable fortress. The defences of Tailleville stretched out into the cornfields in front of the village and were linked back to the château with trenches and tunnels. Built into the wall towards its western end were two pill-boxes. One was a Tobruk machine-gun post and the other, right on the far end of the wall, was a large steep-sided mortar pit. As it approached the village C Company came under heavy fire from snipers and mortars in the wooded area around the water tower to your left.

Moving along this road with his mortar section was Sergeant Albanie Drapeau of C Company, North Shore Regiment.

'I followed Capt LeBlanc on the way to attack Tailleville and on nearing the village we suddenly came under machine gun fire with the whole of C Company in the open. We were following the road but it was not much protection. The O.C. called for mortar fire on the enemy position and Capt leBlanc showed me the exact clump of trees he wanted the mortar fire to be brought down on. Luckily I made a quick correction in degrees and the first ranging rounds fell exactly where he wanted them. In a few minutes the mortars had quietened the German machine guns. Luck was with me that day for each time I was able to score direct hits. The village was a strongpoint and the fight went on all the afternoon as the whole German garrison was dug in underground, first aid posts, garages, stables, everything, and tunnels to every place.'

Source: Will R. Bird, *The North Shore (New Brunswick) Regiment*, p. 220.

The château at Tailleville. *(Author)*

The Tailleville château still shows signs of the struggle that took place during its capture. *(Author)*

Lt-Col Buell, the North Shore Regiment CO, then brought his A Company across to the right to make a battalion attack, with his HQ party going down the centre of the road. A few tanks from the Fort Garry Horse also joined the move. The North Shore men were mortared and shelled all the way across the open ground and Buell and his team were forced off the road to the east, Buell having to crawl through the grain to keep below the fierce enemy fire.

DIRECTIONS: Drive on into the village and look along the line of the wall to see the two pill-boxes. Turn right into the courtyard of the château. The grounds now host some builders' yards so you can park inside the walls without being intrusive.

THE SITE: The large entrance you have come through was blown by Fort Garry Horse tanks during the attack and this is where C Company made a breach into the grounds. The area around the château was a maze of trenches and dug-outs, with numerous buried resistance posts and machine-gun nests. Snipers

BATTLEFIELD TOURS

continued to fire from the building and through slit holes in the walls surrounding the grounds into the afternoon making progress towards the château very costly, not only for the troops in the initial attack, but for the follow-up companies later. Once inside the grounds, the North Shore Regiment had to clear all the trenches and buildings. In the early afternoon it was announced that the area was free, but this was premature because firing soon broke out once more and the whole site had to be swept again. It was not until early evening, after four complete sweeps of the grounds, that the area was finally declared safe. The costly capture of this fortress delayed the North Shore Regiment's move inland and its attack against the radar station 2 km to the south.

Walk across to the wall surrounding the grounds. About 80 metres left of the entrance one of the slits in the wall can be seen.

Firing slit in the wall of the grounds of the château at Tailleville. *(Author)*

This gave good observation all the way to St-Aubin. There are others some distance further along to the left. For those who would like to examine the pill-boxes on the outside of the wall, go back out the entrance, turn left and make your way along the edge of the field alongside the wall. This can be awkward, especially after the field has been ploughed. Inspection of the bunkers will show that access to them was directly through the stone wall into the grounds.

Retrace your steps into the courtyard and across to the château. Look carefully and you can see the damage caused to the building during the attack. None of the defence works are now visible in the grounds.

DIRECTIONS: Drive out of the entrance and turn right. Follow the road around to the right and then left; pull over safely. Walk back to the gateway to the farm you have just passed. Note the almost completely buried Tobruk machine-gun post on the left.

THE SITE: The gateway is the entrance to le Ferme du Prieuré, which forms part of the complex of buildings surrounding the château. In this gateway, whilst giving orders to Major

McNaughton of A Company and a party of his men, Lt-Col Buell came under fire from very close quarters. A machine gun in a weapons pit nearby opened up on the group killing three of the men including the major. One signaller lay wounded in the road. He was pulled to cover by Buell and they both then had to endure more machine-gun fire and a host of grenades thrown from the post until a Fort Garry Horse tank came around the corner behind them to give them cover. An attack was then put in from the opposite direction and the machine-gun post wiped out. In the farm at the time was the farmer, Felix Cassignuel. Unfortunately he was killed later that afternoon by a Canadian grenade. His death is commemorated on the memorial at the southern entrance to the village. The farm is now run by his grandson, also called Felix Cassignuel.

The farm of le Prieuré at Tailleville. Lt-Col Buell was pinned down in its gateway by fire from the Tobruk machine-gun pit in the foreground. *(Author)*

It took most of the afternoon to clear the village and it was almost nightfall before the North Shore Regiment could finally declare Tailleville free of Germans. Buell was then ordered to make contact with the Régiment la Chaudière in Bény and dig in for the night, ready to move against the radar station at first light.

DIRECTIONS: Continue to the junction with the D35. Turn right and then take the next left after about 100 metres, past the memorial to the dead of the village killed during the fighting, on

Tailleville

R12 H2

R15

R9 H1 B1

? ROCKET
PROJECTORS

CURED EMPLACEMENT
RPOSE UNKNOWN

R12 H2 T

WASSERMAN

ERT:- ?C·P·

R10 H1

WK

R10

3

R12

R13

0   250   500

Metres

R16 H1

British 1944 map showing the anticipated German defences around Tailleville and the Douvres radar station. (Base maps: GSGS 4347 Creully 37/18SE and St-Aubin 40/18SW, Stop Press edition, 20 May 1944, showing (in purple) German positions as appreciated by Allies and (in red) most recent Allied intelligence) the D219 towards Basly. Drive for around 1 km, until you are alongside a large wood on the right and open ground on the left.

THE SITE: Look to the fields on the left and notice the large mounds over concrete bunkers. These are the positions of the northern part of the Douvres radar station. When the North Shore Regiment began its move south from Tailleville on the morning of 7 June, the plan was to attack from the wood on the right, but as soon as the leading infantry began to move out of the village, they came under fire from this wood. Lt-Col Buell deployed C Company to clear the area, but it found that the wood was honey-combed with trenches and prepared positions. Progress in clearing these was extremely slow, so a further company was sent into the wood to help. This delayed the attack on the radar station until late afternoon. By then, some support had been taken from the battalion to fight off the counter-attack being made further to the south against 9th Canadian Infantry Brigade by 12th SS Panzer Division. By the time Buell had finally deployed his men and got the tanks and 19th Field Regiment in position to support his attack, reconnaissance had found that his force lacked sufficient strength to capture the site. Brigadier Blackader agreed that the fortified area was more than one battalion could handle and called off the attack. Elements of 51st

The earth-covered bunkers that made up the northern part of the radar station at Douvres. This sector housed the tall *Wassermann* long-range detection radar antenna and was separated from the southern sector by the road that runs from Bény to Douvres. *(Author)*

(Highland) Division had by then landed on Mike Beach and 5th Battalion, Black Watch, and other units were given the task of taking the radar station. The North Shore Regiment then moved to Anguerny to help anchor the east of the Canadian lodgement.

DIRECTIONS: Continue to the junction and turn left towards Douvres-la-Délivrande. After a few hundred metres you pass between the northern and southern parts of the radar station; large grass topped bunkers can be clearly seen on both sides of the road. Find a suitable place to stop and pull over.

THE SITE: 5th Black Watch did not attack the radar station on 7 June, for it, like the North Shore Regiment, found that the position was much too strong. Specialised armour from 80th Assault Squadron, RE, part of 79th Armoured Division, probed around the perimeter but lost three AVREs on mines and suffered some damage to other tanks from anti-tank guns. For the next ten days the garrison was kept sealed inside by 46 and 48 RM Commandos. On 17 June, after careful preparations, the station was subjected to a set-piece armoured attack by 5th Assault Regiment, RE, supported by 41 RM Commando. The operation began with feint attacks from the west and south by 77th Assault Squadron, RE, followed by a sustained artillery barrage on identified positions by 7.2-inch howitzers and a battery of 105-mm self-propelled guns. The two parts of the station were then attacked by four assault teams each including two flail tanks of 22nd Dragoons and a troop of AVREs from 26th Assault Squadron, RE. The attack on the northern sector was carried out from the woods behind you by one assault team. The other three attacked the more heavily defended southern part of the complex.
DIRECTIONS: Drive on to the junction a few hundred metres ahead and turn right. This was the area of the forming-up point for the southern assault teams. The flail tanks moved from here into the cornfields to the south-west, driving straight for the radar station. Follow the road round to the right and stop safely.

THE SITE: You are now in the position of the outer wire and protective minefield of the station fortress. The armoured attack went in across the ground to your right. Once the Crabs had cleared the outer minefield and wire they moved aside and let the AVREs through into the compound. These then attacked the concrete fortifications with their bunker-busting petard mortars and their crews laid 70-lb 'beehive' explosive charges against the armoured doors and reinforced roofs of the shelters. Then the troops of 41 RM Commando were let loose on the trenches and shelters to winkle out stubborn German defenders. The garrison, mostly *Luftwaffe* personnel, soon realised that further resistance was pointless and surrendered. Allied casualties were relatively light, with just three men killed and seven wounded.

Bomb damage done to one of the underground chambers within the radar station at Douvres. *(IWM B6314)*

Sergeant Sorensen of 26th Assault Squadron, RE, took part in the attack in his AVRE across the ground to your right.

'The AVRE in front of me succeeded in getting its offside track in a deep trench and was stuck there immobile. My commander gave me the order to overtake on the left. As I did so there was a terrific concussion and my whole vehicle gave a lurch. My instrument panel lights went out as well as all the interior lights. My first impression was that we had hit a mine, and I tried the steering to see if the tracks were intact. As I did I saw my co-driver lying with a terrible wound in his head. He was unmistakably dead, and I realised we had been hit by a shell. The next moment the whole of the driving compartment caught fire. I was almost suffocated by flame, but managed to open the hatch above my head enough to scramble through. As I was scrambling out the ammunition in the hull Besa was exploding and a piece of shrapnel hit me in the leg. I jumped clear and ran for a bomb crater about fifteen yards away. As I jumped into it I was joined by my wireless operator and my gunner. Hardly had we dropped into it than my tank blew up. The force of the explosion may be gathered from the fact that the turret, which weighs about ten tons, was later found fifty yards away.'

Source: Anon., *Royal Engineers Battlefield Tour: Normandy to the Seine*, p. 120.

DIRECTIONS: Continue down the road and pull into the car park of the radar station on the right.

THE SITE: The museum is now administered by the *Mémorial de Caen (see p. 105 for contact details)* and is open only on certain days in summer. Only the southern section and the buildings within the present wire perimeter are accessible; the rest of the former radar station is on private land.

The Douvres radar station was the largest to be set up in Calvados by the *Luftwaffe*. It was code-named *Distelfink* ('Goldfinch') and formed part of the continuous chain of Atlantic Wall radar detection stations. The 25-acre site was split into two: the smaller northern sector housed the Siemens *Wassermann* long range detection antenna, while the larger southern sector had two Telefunken *Würzburg* short range and two Telefunken *Freya* medium range aerials. The two areas held over 30 concrete works and the overall perimeter was surround by anti-tank obstacles, wire and minefields. Inside this ring the bunkers were linked by trenches and protected with more wire and anti-personnel minefields. The base was a complete fortress, surrounded by machine guns, anti-tank and field guns and anti-aircraft weapons. The station was commanded by *Leutnant* (2nd Lieutenant) Igle and was held by 8th Company, 53rd Air Force Regiment. The garrison and operations staff comprised around 200 men and 36 radar control officers. The garrison was reinforced later by men of 8th and 12th Companies, 736th Grenadier Regiment, when

Two soldiers from I British Corps stand beside the graves of a British and a German soldier who were killed during the battle for the radar station at Douvres. The picture was taken in the northern compound alongside the remains of a *Wassermann* Type M long-range radar aerial. *(IWM B6301)*

they fell back from Tailleville during the North Shore Regiment's attack on the village. A few troops from 192nd Panzergrenadier Regiment also found their way into the fortress when their abortive drive to the sea failed during the evening of D-Day.

A visit to the inside of the radar station is to be recommended, for it houses an interesting exhibition on the development of radar and gives access to several of the bunkers. If it is open you will be able to walk through an important site associated with the invasion and explore contemporary buildings that saw a great deal of action. If you visit out of season there is still much to see from outside the compound. The highlight of the visit inside is the 20-roomed *Anton* bunker built on two levels, which contains a reconstructed *Seeburg* plotting table and other refurbished rooms and displays. Also of great interest is the giant *Würzburg Riese* radar with its 7.5-metre diameter parabolic antenna and operating cabin. This example was captured elsewhere at the end of the war and given to the French by the British for research purposes. The aerial was used for many years in pioneering work in the field of radio-astronomy and was installed here in 1994.

Corridor leading to the communications room in the CP L479 *Anton* bunker of the radar station. This blockhouse is the largest on the site. *(Author)*

DIRECTIONS: (The following directions outline the most convenient route to the Douvres War Cemetery for those with cars. Cyclists should consult a good map and take a much shorter, if more complex, route back down the road through the town of Douvres.) Turn right out of the car park and continue to the junction with the D404. Turn left and drive towards Caen for about 2 km until the roundabout. Go around the roundabout taking the fourth exit towards Douvres north along the D7 for 2 km. Continue straight on at the next roundabout and then take the right turning just past the Douvres la Déliverande War Cemetery. Park and walk back to the main entrance.

THE SITE: Most of the men buried here died during the early fighting and the invasion itself. The cemetery contains 1,125 burials, of which 927 are British, 11 Canadian, 3 Australian, 1 Polish and 182 German. Only one of those interred remains unidentified.

THIS IS THE END OF THE TOUR: To return to Courseulles or Caen, go back down the D7 road to the large roundabout and turn right for Courseulles, or go straight ahead along the dual carriageway for Caen.

TOUR E

BATTLES WITH THE HITLERJUGEND DIVISION

OBJECTIVE: This tour starts with 7th Canadian Infantry Brigade's drive inland and then visits the sites of the subsequent 12th SS Panzer Division counter-attacks against 3rd Canadian Infantry Division.

DURATION/SUITABILITY: The tour covers some 48 km and will take at least half a day to complete. It is good for the cyclist with quiet roads and interesting countryside; there are some hilly sections, but not of long duration. It is excellent for the disabled; all sites are accessible by car.

DIRECTIONS: Start the tour by the harbour at Courseulles opposite the DD Sherman as for *Tour A*. Head inland following the road around by the harbour. Continue past the swing bridge on the right and take the second turning on the left. Go up past the château to the junction and turn right. After about 100 metres the road swings to the left and rises to a roundabout. Take the second exit towards Caen, the D79c, and continue to the next roundabout. Take the first exit, the D170 towards Reviers. Continue across open countryside and pass through Reviers to the roundabout in its centre. Continue straight on by the D170 towards Fontaine-Henry. The road passes through some pleasant countryside along the Mue valley, with occasional picnic tables set out among the trees lining the route. Just before Fontaine-Henry is the village of Moulineaux. Over on the left, beyond the trees, was the site of the German field gun battery to the west of Bény attacked by the Régiment la Chaudière during the afternoon of D-Day. Continue along the D170 into Fontaine-Henry itself, taking note to keep right at a fork in the road following the direction Thaon. Follow the road around to the right and on the left is the entry to the magnificent château of Fontaine-Henry, with the Renaissance house itself clearly visible from the road. If your tour coincides with its opening times, it is well worth a visit. Otherwise carry on up the hill to the church and pull over safely.

e Authie memorial to the North Nova
Scotia Highlanders
f Rots church
g Monument to 46 RM Commando
h Bretteville l'Orgueilleuse memorial
to the Regina Rifles
i Secqueville-en-Bessin War Cemetery
j Putot-en-Bessin memorial to
1st Canadian Scottish
k Brouay War Cemetery
l Audrieu memorial to Canadians
massacred by 12th SS Panzer Division
m Le Mesnil-Patry memorial to
the Queen's Own Rifles
n Norrey-en-Bessin memorial
o End of tour
p Carpiquet airfield

Base map: IGN 1612OT

Tanks moving through the narrow streets of Thaon on the drive inland from the beaches. *(Frank L. Dubervill, NAC PA-133749)*

THE SITE: Nearby is the memorial to the Régiment de la Chaudière and the Regina Rifles who liberated the village. The area around the church was the scene of much fighting with several men killed in the churchyard, including the commander of B Company, Regina Rifles, Major Peters. On the outside wall of the church, to the left as you go through the gate, is a plaque listing the 11 Canadians who lost their lives in the liberation.

DIRECTIONS: Continue towards Thaon, still on the D170. The road passes out into open countryside with the valley of the River Mue on the left. As you approach Thaon, with its distinctive church steeple towering above the village, over to the left you can see the wall surrounding Thaon's château, the Régiment de la Chaudière's headquarters on D-Day. Continue into Thaon to the crossroads in the centre of the village. Turn left and motor for around 300 metres. In the middle of an island on the left is a memorial to 10th Canadian Armoured Regiment (The Fort Garry Horse) whose tanks supported 7th Canadian Infantry Brigade on its drive inland up the Mue valley.

Turn around and go back to the crossroads, turning left to continue along the D170 towards Cairon. After about 2 km you come to a junction. Turn left on to the D22 and proceed down the hill past the church into Cairon. Pass around several bends looking out for the road to the right on the far side of the village, sign-posted Rosel and Rots. Turn right here on to a continuation of the D170 noting the stone tablet on the right, which remembers those who liberated the village on 6 June 1944. Continue for just over 1 km to the junction just after you enter the outskirts of Rosel. Turn left on to the D126 towards Caen.

THE SITE: On the evening of D-Day this was the limit of 7th Canadian Infantry Brigade's advance. By that time 9th Canadian Infantry Brigade had reached Villons-les-Buissons, 3 km to the north-east, and 8th Canadian Infantry Brigade was established further back towards the beaches, providing the rearguard after the assault earlier that morning. Over to the right (south) is open country leading down to Carpiquet airfield about 4 km away. The airfield was one of 3rd Canadian Infantry Division's key D-Day objectives. Although Maj-Gen Keller and his men did not know it, there was no appreciable body of Germans between this point and Carpiquet that night. Even the airfield itself had been abandoned by its garrison. More than four weeks were to pass before the Canadians finally took the airfield.

DIRECTIONS: Continue for just over 4 km along the D126 road, then, just at the entrance to Cussy, turn right and go into the village. Take the next road on the left and carry on to a roundabout. Leave it at the second exit, sign-posted to Abbaye d'Ardennes. Motor on a short distance and stop.

THE SITE: Ahead and to the left is the medieval abbey of Ardennes, the advance headquarters of SS-Colonel Kurt Meyer's 25th SS Panzergrenadier Regiment from 7 June 1944. The abbey is surrounded by a high stone wall with its range of buildings grouped around the abbey's ancient church. Meyer arrived late on D-Day and immediately went to visit GenLt Richter, at his HQ in the quarries at la Folie, just 2 km to the east. There Meyer received telephone orders from Fritz Witt, 12th SS Panzer Division's commander, to launch an attack against the beachhead the next day in concert with 21st Panzer Division. Meyer was to use those elements of 12th SS Panzer Division that had arrived in the area. The attack was to begin at 1600 hours on 7 June.

BATTLEFIELD TOURS

Meyer's staff had meanwhile selected the abbey as his regiment's advance HQ and were directing all units of the division that had arrived to this point. Meyer's actual HQ that night was in a café 1 km south at St-Germain-la-Blanche-Herbe.

Motor straight on and pass to the right of the stone wall surrounding the abbey complex. On the left can be seen the main

Memorial to the Canadians who were murdered by soldiers of 12th SS Panzer Division. It was erected on the site of the massacre in the garden at the rear of the abbey buildings at Ardennes. (Author)

gateway to the abbey courtyard and a plaque which commemorates the 18 Canadians murdered by men of 12th SS Panzer Division within its walls. On 7 June and on various subsequent days, prisoners were taken into a small garden adjacent to the courtyard and shot in cold blood. The abbey is now a private dwelling place and visitors are only admitted by invitation. Please respect the privacy of those who live there.

DIRECTIONS: Turn around and head back the way you have come and then turn right to pass along the northern side of the abbey. The north gateway to the abbey, the scene of much coming and going during June 1944, is 100 metres on. Continue to the far end of the abbey wall and pull over where safe.

THE SITE: The curtain wall surrounding the abbey was much damaged during the subsequent fighting and a good view of the buildings can now be obtained through one of the many gaps in the stonework. The church is undergoing a prolonged period of restoration to bring it back to its original condition. At each corner of the church are prominent towers, which served as vantage points for German commanders and artillery observers.

DIRECTIONS: Turn around and go back along the abbey walls. Follow the road round to the right and pull over after 100 metres.

THE SITE: Ahead of you is the village of Cussy, across to the left (north-west) is Authie and further round to the west is Franqueville. During the morning of 7 June, 9th Canadian

The church of Ardennes abbey. It was from one of the towers on the right of the building that *SS-Standartenführer* Meyer watched 7th Canadian Infantry Brigade's advance through Buron and Authie, before he launched his attack. *(Author)*

Infantry Brigade resumed its move to the south from Villons-les-Buissons, through Buron and Authie and on to Franqueville. Tanks of the Sherbrooke Fusiliers led the advance, carrying the infantry of the North Nova Scotia Highlanders with them on their backs. The Highlanders occupied Authie and Buron with little opposition, with the Sherbrooke Fusiliers Shermans sweeping wide around on the flanks of the villages. By 1400 hours the tanks had reached the hamlet of Franqueville. The moves had been made against little opposition; only stragglers from Richter's 716th Infantry Division were there to oppose the Canadians. Even so, the Allied troops came under increasing fire from the area to their left as Meyer's battlegroup continued building up its strength.

Watching these movements from his vantage point in one of the towers of the abbey church was Meyer himself. He could not believe his luck; the Canadians were advancing right across the face of his gathering force, unaware of the presence of the tanks and guns overlooking them. It was an opportunity too good to miss. Meyer decided not to wait until 1600 hours but to launch his attack there and then. The Canadians were caught completely by surprise and were attacked in their exposed flank by 2nd Battalion, 25th SS Panzergrenadier Regiment, passing over the ground in front of you. Tanks of 5th Company, 12th SS Panzer Regiment, moved against Franqueville to your left rear and then swung around the far side of Authie. To your right, more Panzer IVs from 7th Company, 12th SS Panzer Regiment, attacked from east of Cussy towards Buron. Further over to the east, Meyer's 1st Battalion, 25th SS Panzergrenadier Regiment, attacked towards 3rd British Infantry Division at Cambes-en-Plaine. The Canadians were caught off guard and suffered heavy casualties. They were driven back through Authie and Buron almost as far back as their start line at Villons-les-Buissons.

DIRECTIONS: Continue to the roundabout and take the third exit along the D220c towards Authie. Carry on over the next roundabout and into the village. Go straight on at the crossroads in the centre of Authie and immediately stop in the small car park on the right. Walk across the road to the monument behind you.

THE SITE: The memorial commemorates the fierce fighting that took place in the village and the baptism of fire suffered by the North Nova Scotia Highlanders. The houses all around are for the most part post-war; almost all of the buildings here were destroyed in the fighting in 1944. The area along the main street and around the church was the scene of vicious hand-to-hand fighting and was also the location of the start of the atrocities committed by 12th SS Panzer Division. Many Canadians who had surrendered and were helpless were shot or bayoneted to death in cold blood by the side of the road.

DIRECTIONS: Continue up past the church and out into the countryside to the west of the village. Follow the road through several twists and turns and then round a sharp left hand bend. Drive on to the next junction and stop safely.

THE SITE: Over to the left and slightly in front of you is the hamlet of Franqueville. It was in this village that the armour of 12th SS Panzer Regiment caught the tanks of the Sherbrooke Fusiliers' advance guard in their left flank, annihilating the whole troop. The panzers then swept towards your present location to

Panzergrenadiers and tanks from 3rd Company, 12th SS Panzer Regiment, pull back through Villeneuve after their abortive attack on Bretteville-l'Orgueilleuse during the night of 8–9 June. *(Bundesarchiv 146/1976/100/09)*

get to the western side of Authie. They continued their attack towards Gruchy and Buron.

Now turn right and motor out across the open fields, heading for the church spire at Rots. To your left, 1 km away, is the Caen–Bayeux highway with Carpiquet airfield just beyond. After 12th SS Panzer Division's attack had stalled on 7 June, it was ordered to attack west to eliminate the Canadian salient that had formed beyond the Caen–Bayeux highway and to prevent the capture of Carpiquet airfield. On 8 June 25th SS Panzergrenadier Regiment, supported by Panther tanks, attacked from around Ardennes abbey along the highway towards Bretteville-l'Orgueilleuse. In doing so the Germans passed through the small village of Villeneuve, which is ahead of you and to the left.

DIRECTIONS: Continue into Rots and stop by the church.

THE SITE: This village was the scene of much bitter fighting on 11 June when elements of 26th SS Panzergrenadier Regiment, which were holding the village, were attacked by 46 RM Commando supported by Fort Garry Horse tanks. A tank battle between a German Panther and some Canadian Shermans took place in the small square here alongside the church. Intense fighting between panzergrenadiers and marines continued all day in the roads and houses in the village with fearful casualties.

An historian with the Régiment de la Chaudière described the scene when he entered the village after the battle.

'The commandos lie dead in rows beside the dead SS. Grenades are scattered all over the road and in the porches of the houses. Here we see a commando and an SS man, literally dead in each others' arms, having slaughtered each other. There, a German and a Canadian tank have engaged each other to destruction, and are still smouldering, and from each blackened turret hangs the charred corpse of a machine gunner. Over here, are a group who ran towards a wall for shelter, and were shot down before they got there. And then, near the church, as the advance guard of C Company and the carriers turn the corner, there are three Germans. Only three, but one of them instantly draws his pistol and hits one of our men. A Bren gunner kills two of the three SS men, but the survivor does not surrender, he dodges us and gets away.'

Source: Alexander McKee, *Caen, Anvil of Victory*, p. 93.

DIRECTIONS: Turn left and motor 50 metres to a stop sign. Turn right here and a short distance along on the right is a memorial stone to those lost in the fighting in the village. Continue over the bridge across the diminutive River Mue, up the hill and turn left at the top into Chemin du Hamel.

THE SITE: This is one axis of 46 RM Commando's attack against the SS panzergrenadiers in Rots, one which ground to a halt in the hamlet of le Hamel. After around 500 metres you come to a memorial on the right, which remembers those of the commando lost in the battle. Alongside is a plaque listing the names of the 22 Royal Marines who died in Rots and le Hamel.

DIRECTIONS: Continue past the water tower and stop just outside the village.

A Canadian armoured scout car knocked out during the battle to capture Rots. *(Frank L. Dubervill, NAC PA-132437)*

THE SITE: A short distance ahead is the old Caen–Bayeux road, now bereft of heavy traffic since the opening of a dual carriageway to the south. In 1944 it was the Route National 13 (RN13) but now it is downgraded to the D83c. To the left is Rots and to the right is the prominent steeple of the church at Bretteville-l'Orgueilleuse. On the night of 8–9 June, a battlegroup consisting of three companies of Panther tanks from *Obersturmbannführer* Max Wünsche's 12th SS Panzer Regiment and troops from 1st Battalion, 25th SS Panzergrenadier Regiment, attacked Bretteville-l'Orgueilleuse from the east, using the Caen–Bayeux highway as its axis. The objective was to remove the Canadians from their salient over the RN13 and then use the area for a massed attack by 12th SS Panzer Division and Panzer Lehr Division up the Mue and Seulles valleys. One company of Panther tanks advanced along the main road, while the two other companies moved through the fields on either side. All were carrying panzergrenadiers from Meyer's regiment on their hulls. The defenders of the village were from the Regina Rifles. They were protected by a screen of 6-pounder anti-tank guns and supported by a regiment of field artillery. The attack was pressed home with great bravery by the young SS troops, but was finally beaten off. The anti-tank guns took a great toll of the German armour. At one time the whole of Bretteville was virtually surrounded by tanks and panzergrenadiers, all looking for a way to break through the defences. Two Panthers got into the town almost to the Regina Rifles HQ beside the church. The first was knocked out by an infantryman with his PIAT anti-tank weapon at 15 metres range. The other retreated back towards Rots.

DIRECTIONS: Go on to the road junction and turn right.

THE SITE: You are now on the axis of the 12th SS Panzer Division attack. About 200 metres short of Bretteville were the positions of B Company, Regina Rifles, with the anti-tank guns to the right of the road. It was about here that the first of the attacking Panther tanks was knocked out and the panzer-grenadiers travelling with them dismounted and attacked the Canadians, forcing B Company back into the village.

DIRECTIONS: Go into Bretteville and pull over just before the church and the traffic lights in the centre. On the left, alongside the church, is a farmhouse with white railings set back from the street. This was the Regina Rifles HQ and it was almost opposite this point that a Panther tank was knocked out with a PIAT.

Lt-Col Matheson's HQ in the farm in Bretteville-l'Orgueilleuse. *(Author)*

Top: A knocked-out Panther tank from 12th SS Panzer Regiment in the centre of Bretteville right opposite the entrance to the Regina Rifles HQ. *(IWM B6232)*

Above: The three intrepid PIAT gunners who knocked out the Panther inspect their prey. *(Donald I. Grant, NAC PA-116529)*

Go on through the traffic lights for around 300 metres and turn right into Place des Canadiens (sign-posted la Poste). Follow the road round the square to the monument opposite the French war memorial where a tablet commemorates the Regina Rifles' sacrifice in defending the village. Return to the main road and turn right. Continue for about 200 metres and take the next turn on the right, the D93 towards Secqueville-en-Bessin. The road passes out of Bretteville through a few twists and turns into open country. Secqueville is 2 km further on. Go into the village to the crossroads and turn right, following the sign to the Secqueville Commonwealth War Cemetery. After half a kilometre take the sign-posted track on the left. The cemetery is ahead on the left.

THE SITE: This is one of the most exposed and desolate of all the Normandy cemeteries, located some way from the village and surrounded by open wind-swept fields. Inside the graveyard all is neat, tidy and peaceful as ever, but its location means that, sadly, it gets very few visitors. There are 99 British burials here; one is unknown. There are 18 German graves. Most of the British are from the West Country county regiments of 43rd (Wessex) Division and appear to have been killed in early July during the offensive against Hill 112, 12 km to the south. Why these men should have been brought here for burial is a mystery

DIRECTIONS: Return into Secqueville-en-Bessin.

THE SITE: On the night of D-Day, 7th Canadian Infantry Brigade reached Cainet and le Fresne-Camilly, 3–4 km to the north/north-west. On 7 June it continued its advance to Secqueville. The Regina Rifles moved on to Bretteville and the Winnipeg Rifles pushed forward to Putot-en-Bessin, both battalions finally reaching their D-Day objectives.

DIRECTIONS: Turn left at the crossroads in the village and head south on the D217, ensuring that you follow the road to the right on the outskirts of Secqueville. Continue along the D217, across two roundabouts and over the Caen–Bayeux highway. Take the next left after the second roundabout towards Putot-en-Bessin. Follow the road into the village and then take the left fork opposite the telephone box that leads up to the church (Rue de l'Église). Carry on past the church and park on the right.

BATTLEFIELD TOURS

Well-camouflaged soldiers from 12th SS Panzer Division man a light anti-tank gun in the fields inland from the landings. *(Bundesarchiv 146/1982/111/31A)*

THE SITE: Here is a monument dedicated to the 1st Battalion, Canadian Scottish. The Winnipeg Rifles took Putot-en-Bessin on 7 June but the village was lost early the next day in 26th SS Panzergrenadier Regiment's murderous counter-attack. The Winnipeg Rifles defended the line of the railway to the south and were attacked over open fields in the early hours of 8 June from the direction of le Mesnil-Patry. After much hard fighting the battalion was overrun and had to withdraw. The Winnipeg Rifles suffered 256 casualties that day, of whom 105 were killed. Many of those who survived the onslaught were captured and were forced to endure further punishment at the hands of their captors of the Hitler Youth. 1st Canadian Scottish retook the village that evening, but also suffered many casualties, including 45 killed.

DIRECTIONS: Return back down the road and turn left at the junction by the phone box. Continue south through the village, round the right hand bend at the end of the main street and out of Putot. At the next junction turn left and go over the rail bridge, the scene of much fighting during the German attack as both sides fought desperately to hold this strategically important crossing over the cutting. Once over the railway turn immediately right along the D94 into Brouay. Take the second turning on the right after about 500 metres and follow the sign to Brouay Commonwealth War Cemetery. Go under the railway bridge and round to the right to the church. Walk through the churchyard to the British cemetery at the rear (if the main gate is locked, there is a small gate at the side of the churchyard to the left).

THE SITE: You have now passed out of the Juno Beach zone into the area proper to 50th (Northumbrian) Division, which landed on Gold Beach. The graveyard here in Brouay has 377 burials, of which just seven are unknown. Most of the graves are those of men killed during the advance from Gold Beach to this area and in the subsequent operations to expand the lodgement.

DIRECTIONS: Go back into Brouay. At the main road in the village turn right. Carry on along the D94 for 3 km into Audrieu, turn left and pull over opposite the church by a section of wall with a large plaque.

THE SITE: The road you have travelled along was that taken by

Memorial at Audrieu to the Canadian prisoners of war who were killed nearby. *(Author)*

a group of over 20 Canadians who were taken prisoner at Putot-en-Bessin by the SS panzergrenadiers. They were marched through Brouay into Audrieu, taken past this point and into the grounds of the château of Audrieu, which lies a little way away to the right of the monument through the trees. Here they were massacred by reconnaissance troops of 12th SS Panzer Division. The monument lists those who were murdered in this and other atrocities.

DIRECTIONS: Continue for a few hundred metres for a good view of the château on the left, now a hotel. Turn around and go back through Brouay to the junction with the D217 near the railway bridge. Turn right and after 400 metres turn left towards le Mesnil-Patry. The ground to the left is that over which 2nd Battalion, 26th SS Panzergrenadiers, attacked the Winnipeg Rifles

BATTLEFIELD TOURS

Prisoners from 12th SS Panzer Division. *(Ken Bell, NAC PA-131397)*

in Putot in the dark early hours of 8 June. Continue into the village and turn right at the road junction. After a short distance, pass by the church and pull over opposite the monument.

The memorial is to the Queen's Own Rifles of Canada and 6th Canadian Armoured Regiment (1st Hussars) who fought a particularly nasty battle against 12th SS Panzer Division in the village on 11 June, when the 1st Hussars lost 36 tanks and the Rifles had 55 men killed.

Turn your car around and go back past the junction you just came out of towards Norrey-en-Bessin.

THE SITE: The road from Norrey was the axis of the Canadian advance into le Mesnil-Patry. The Canadians attacked through the position held by SS troops in the fields near the edge of the village and then met tanks and anti-tank guns in the village.

> **On the edge of le Mesnil-Patry was *Pionier* (Sapper) Horst Lütgens, stalking a Canadian tank with his panzerfaust.**
>
> 'Gathering all my courage I jumped out of my hole and crawled close to the ground, while machine gun salvos whistled above. I was suddenly very calm, but a rage quelled [*sic*] inside me. I asked myself what had happened to my comrades up front. Were they dead or had they let

the tanks roll past? Then I looked for a victim. There it sat, the Sherman, looking huge and mighty. Its turret was pointed in the direction of our battalion command post. Its gun fired round after round. I had to get closer to it. I started to crawl. Now there were even more tanks! One, two, three, four, five of these Shermans could be seen in the blue haze of the air saturated by gunpowder smoke. When I was within twenty metres, I aimed and fired. But nothing happened. Jam! Just what I needed. Once more, I cocked and fired. Jammed again! Now I was getting nervous. I cocked the weapon again and this time it roared off. I could not watch the hit. The tank providing cover had spotted me and was firing on me. I did hear the explosion.'

Source: Hubert Meyer, *The History of the 12. SS Panzerdivision 'Hitlerjugend'*, p. 69.

DIRECTIONS: Continue across the open fields towards Norrey-en-Bessin (sign-posted St-Manvieu-Norrey) and carry on to the crossroads. Go across and into the parking area opposite the church. Nearby is a monument commemorating those killed in the fighting in the village. Continue eastwards to the junction with the D83 and turn left towards Bretteville-l'Orgueilleuse.

THE SITE: The open ground to the right was the scene of another of 12th SS Panzer Division's attacks against the Canadians holding this salient over the RN13, when Max Wünsche's Panthers from 12th SS Panzer Regiment advanced along the southern side of the railway line and attempted to strike the flanks of 8th Canadian Infantry Brigade in Norrey-en-Bessin. As the Germans approached the area near the railway bridge up ahead they in turn were caught in their flanks by tanks and anti-tank guns in Bretteville and lost seven Panthers and some supporting infantry. This failure led the panzer division to reconsider its tactics and assume a defensive role while more divisions were moved into the area against the Allied lodgement.

THIS IS THE END OF THE TOUR: Carry on over the railway bridge to the roundabout. Take the second exit, sign-posted Caen. This dual carriageway will link into the Caen ring road (the *Periphérique*). Exit at Junction 5 to return to Courseulles.

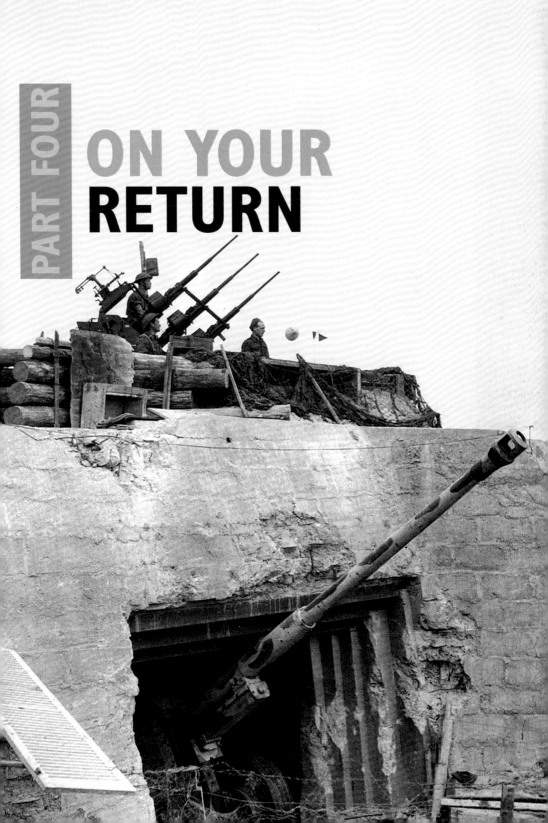

PART FOUR

ON YOUR
RETURN

FURTHER RESEARCH

If you have undertaken the battlefield tours outlined in the book and are intrigued to know more about the landings on Juno Beach, there are several places to visit in England and numerous books to read which will give you a fuller understanding of the action.

Many of the troops who landed on Juno Beach left from Southampton and were housed in camps nearby. The hards and quays where troops and equipment were loaded remain, as do the berths in the old and new docks where the ships of the great armada embarked. Southampton also has thriving maritime and aviation museums. Further along the coast in Hampshire is the naval base of Portsmouth. There is now an excellent museum dedicated to the Normandy landings situated along the seafront from Portsmouth Dockyard at Southsea. The *D-Day Museum* is open throughout the year and has an interesting range of items on display including tanks and weapons. A little further along the coast is the *Royal Marines Museum* at Eastney.

Useful Addresses

D–Day Museum and Overlord Embroidery, Clarence Esplanade, Southsea PO5 3NT; tel: 023 9282 7261; email: <info@ddaymuseum.co.uk>. .

Royal Marines Museum Southsea, PO4 9PX; tel: 023 9281 9385; email: <info@royalmarinesmuseum.co.uk>.

Imperial War Museum, Lambeth Road London, SE1 6HZ; tel: 020 7416 5320; email: <mail@iwm.org.uk>; web: <www.iwm.org.uk>.

UK National Archives, Public Record Office, Kew, Richmond, Surrey TW9 4DU; tel: 020 8876 3444; email: <enquiry@nationalarchives.gov.uk>; web: <www.nationalarchives.gov.uk>.

University of Keele Air Photo Library, Keele University, Keele, Staffordshire ST5 5BG; tel/fax: 01782 583395; web: <evidenceincamera.co.uk>.

Public Archives of Canada, 395 Wellington Street Ottawa, Ontario K1A 0N3; tel: +01 613 9470 391.

US National Archives, The National Archives and Records Administration, 8601 Adelphi Road, College Park MD 20740–6001; tel: +01 866 272 6272; web: <www.archives.gov>.

Above: Würzburg Riese radar antenna at the *Luftwaffe* radar station near Douvres. This particular example, although of wartime vintage, is not original to Douvres, but was brought to the site in 1994 after serving as a radio telescope at a radio-astronomy observatory near Orléans. *(Author)*

Page 185: Captured 88-mm gun casemate at the entrance of Courseulles harbour. The Canadians have used the concrete bunker to house a light anti-aircraft position on its roof. The *Bar de la Mer* and an aquarium are now built over this site at the top of the beach. *(Ken Bell, NAC PA-140856)*

The *Imperial War Museum* in London is another good source of information and exhibits relating to the invasion. The museum also holds the photographic archive of all official war pictures, including cine film. You can visit the photographic reference room by appointment to view the collection or to choose and buy prints from the archive. Pictures can also be ordered by post if you know the negative number. The photographs used in this book are just samples of the thousands of pictures the museum holds relating to the fighting in Normandy. Aerial reconnaissance photographs are held at the University of Keele in Staffordshire.

For those who wish to delve deeper into official publications and archives the following might be useful. The Imperial War Museum has copies of all of the official histories of the unitsthat were engaged in the action and these can be consulted in its reading room by appointment. The National Archives at Kew in London (formerly the Public Record Office) holds the war diaries of all the British units which served in Normandy, and has copies of many Canadian ones. This archive also has unpublished after-action reports and summaries of the various battles. Access to this material can be obtained by applying for a reader's ticket.

The internet is another good source of information, although the easily accessible material can be lightweight. One worthwhile site is <www.dday.co.uk>. Also worth pursuing are sites devoted to individual regiments. Type in the name of the regiment on a search engine and browse through the findings.

A broader view of the landings can be gained from the wide range of books published on the invasion. Included here is a select bibliography of some that might be useful:

Anon., *Operation 'Neptune' Landings in Normandy, June 1944*, HMSO, London, 1994.

Anon., *Royal Engineers Battlefield Tour: Normandy to the Seine*, BAOR, 1946.

Anon., *The Story of the 79th British Armoured Division*, Privately Printed, 1946.

Bird, Will R., *The North Shore (New Brunswick) Regiment*, Brunswick Press, Canada, 1963.

Brown, Gordon, & Copp, Terry, *Look To Your Front . . . Regina Rifles*, Wilfred Laurier University, Canada, 2001.

Carell, Paul, *Invasion – They're Coming!*, George Harrap, London, 1962.

Chazette, Alain, *Le Mur de L'Atlantique-en-Normandie*, Heimdal, Bayeux, 2000.

D'Este, Carlo, *Decision in Normandy*, Collins, London, 1983.

Ellis, L.F., *Victory In The West*, HMSO, London, 1962.

Ford, Ken, *D-Day 1944: Gold and Juno Beaches*, Osprey, Oxford, 2002.

Ford, Ken, *D-Day Commando*, Sutton Publishing, Stroud, 2003.

Hastings, Max, *Overlord*, Michael Joseph, London, 1984.

Isby, David C., (ed.), *Fighting The Invasion: The German Army at D-Day*, Greenhill Books, London, 2000.

Marteinson, John, & McNorgan, Michael, *The Royal Canadian Armoured Corps*, RCACA, Ontario, Canada, 2000.

Martin, Charles Cromwell, *Battle Diary*, Dundurn Press, Toronto, 1994.

McKee, Alexander, *Caen: Anvil of Victory*, Souvenir Press, 1964.

Meyer, Hubert, *The History of the 12. SS Panzerdivision 'Hitlerjugend'*, J.J. Fedorowicz, Winnipeg, Canada, 1994.

Portugal, Jean, *We Were There: The Army*, Vol 6, Royal Canadian Military Institute Heritage Society, Ontario, 1998.

Ramsey, Winston G., (ed.), *D-Day Then and Now*, Battle of Britain Prints International, London, 1995.

Saunders, Hilary St-George, *The Green Beret*, Michael Joseph, London, 1949.

INDEX

Page numbers in *italics* denote illustrations.